Love

Jesse

x

THE STORY OF

ROBSON & JEROME

by Bob Ogley

with exclusive photographs from their
musical-comedy TV film

AIN'T MISBEHAVIN'

This is the official book   **Froglets Publications**

Froglets Publications Ltd

Brasted Chart,
Westerham,
Kent TN16 ILY

ISBN
Paperback: 1 872337 83 X
Hardback: 1 872337 81 3

Tel: 01959 562972
Fax: 01959 565365

Front and back cover:
Ain't Misbehavin'
by John Rogers.

This book was originated by Froglets Publications Ltd and printed and bound by Staples Printers (Rochester) Ltd, Neptune Close, Medway City Estate, Rochester, Kent ME2 4LT.

Jacket design and additional artwork by Alison Clarke.

ACKNOWLEDGEMENTS

The author would like to thank the following for their invaluable help in the preparation of this book. Anne Green, Robson Green snr, Phyllida Warner, Eric Flynn, Fern Flynn, Kerry Crellin, Kate Feast, Julie Simpson, Sandra Jobling, Simon Cowell, Norman Stone, Alex Brunner, Anna Jacobs, Barry Ledingham, Fiona Connery, Diana Harris, Holly Aird, Rob Spendlove and Rosie Rowell, the crew and cast of *Ain't Misbehavin'*, the cast of *Casualty*, and, especially, Robson Green and Jerome Flynn.

Photographs from *Soldier, Soldier* reproduced with permission from Carlton UK Television. Photographs by John Rogers, Oliver Upton, Tony Smith and Tony Nutley © Carlton UK Television 1996, pp 49, 50, 53, 58, 59, 62, 63, 65, 71, 73, 76, 86. John Topham Picture Agency p29. London Weekend Television p 45. BBCTV pp 44, 55, 74. Popperfoto p 95. Julie Simpson p 91. Roger Perkins pp 48, 89. Anna Jacobs pp 92, 93. Greenpeace p 82. Peter Wade p 21. RCA pp 1, 5, 69. Anglia TV p 75. Sevenoaks Chronicle p 22. Fern Flynn pp 7, 19, 81, 83, 85, 103 (bottom), 108 (top & bottom right). Central School of Speech and Drama p 41. **Frank Spooner Picture Agency *Ain't Misbehavin'* photographs by John Rogers, copyright reserved pp 99, 100, 101, 103 (top), 104, 105, 106, 107 (both), 108 (bottom left), 109, 110 (all), 111.** Phyllida Warner pp 9 (top), 13, 14, 16 (bottom right), 34, (top right), 54. Mirror Group Newspapers p 84 (bottom). Additional photographs from Robson and Jerome family albums.

CONTENTS

Bob Ogley, a former newspaper editor in Jerome Flynn's home town of Sevenoaks, is the author of a dozen books — two of which have appeared in the national top ten best seller's list. He is a regular contributor to radio and television and lectures frequently to numerous clubs and organisations. Many of his books have supported benevolent and environmental charities, with donations by September, 1996, of more than £90,000.

For information about membership and merchandise please contact the Robson Green & Jerome Flynn Fan Club, PO Box 36, Hexham NE 47 9YZ

Foreword: The Year of Robson and Jerome

IT seemed like a good idea. The band had failed to turn up to a mate's wedding reception so Dave Tucker and Paddy Garvey of the King's Own Fusiliers would take their places and sing the tried-and-tested old favourite *Unchained Melody*. It was another excellent story line in the well-loved TV drama series *Soldier, Soldier.*

Within days of that simple scripted scene at Kate and Kieran's wedding, record shops throughout the country were being inundated with enquiries from *Soldier, Soldier* fans wishing to buy the record. The singing squaddies, played by Robson Green and Jerome Flynn, heard about the fruitless stampede in hundreds of stores and were both flattered and amused. An attractive offer followed from RCA Records to make a record for real. But a "pop" career hadn't figured in their plans for the future. It was all too ludicrous. The answer was definitely "No".

RCA producer Simon Cowell was not going to let the boys escape that easily and, after almost 300 telephone calls to them, their agents, directors and even their mothers, he persuaded them with the help of a tempting offer to go to the recording studios. On May 8th 1995, the 50th anniversary of VE Day, Robson Green and Jerome Flynn released their debut single *Unchained Melody* and *White Cliffs of Dover.* In record shops across the length and breadth of England the single sold as fast as it was delivered, driving many fans to desperation when supplies ran out. Some queued to make sure they could get a copy and there was a scuffle on the floor of Woolworths at Sevenoaks which was not quite in keeping with the spirit of peace and sisterly love on VE Day.

What happened next was extraordinary. Robson and Jerome's record went into the charts at Number One. It stayed there for seven weeks and sold 1.84 million copies to become the fastest selling single of the nineties. RCA Records had got their way and the music business had been turned upside down by two actors who never planned to sing seriously. The pop world was stunned. Some radio stations, including the BBC's Radio One, refused to play the record and music critics turned on the reluctant pair.

But the great British public took no notice. In their hundreds of thousands they continued to invade the shops and by mid-summer of that year Robson and Jerome had sold faster than any record since Band Aid a decade ago and had agreed to release another single and an album for Christmas.

Yet again, to the chagrin and consternation of the blinkered pop world, *I Believe* and *Up on the Roof* went straight in at Number One, stayed there until the end of November, quickly passed the million mark and overtook *Unchained*

Melody as the fastest selling single of the nineties. The debut album, released on November 13th, spent seven weeks at number one in the charts.

Robson and Jerome were now record-breakers extraordinaire. The combined sales of their singles were the highest ever achieved by an act in its debut year and one of the highest of all time. They were the first newcomers to have two Number One singles in the same year since 1981. They had achieved the highest first-week sale (270,000) by a debut album. By Christmas 1995 they had the fastest two-million seller ever.

The boys felt as if they were part of an old MGM musical about the birth of a star. It was like being on a train that started slowly and gathered pace — and there was no way of getting off.

This was the Year of Robson and Jerome and, in some cases, the flak was not flying quite so thickly. One newspaper asked "why do we love them?" and then gave the answer: "Partly because they bring a dash of romance to the lives of love-sick middle-aged women. But mostly because they kept The Beatles off the top of the album charts. Watery versions of clichéd songs selling twice as many albums as the Fab Four. Truly there is a God".

Robson and Jerome were top of the album charts and well behind were The Beatles with their greatly acclaimed *Anthology*. This lovable pair of seasoned actors with an appeal far beyond the teeny-bopper were proving, without doubt, that they could sing — thanks to a musical background in both cases — and their choice of straight, melodic well-loved tracks was not only highly marketable but was attracting a following from five to 95-year-olds who were not the slightest bit interested in the musical snobbery of a resentful pop world.

They had the hostile music media loading and then re-loading their guns and making the most bizarre comments about actors who try to sing. But so what? The singles and the albums sold, not in hundreds, or thousands — but in millions and, according to Simon Cowell, the person who signed the lads for RCA: "They are the nicest people I have ever worked with".

Perhaps that statement alone explains the biggest pop phenomenon of the nineties. This is their story.

A coffee break during the filming of the video for Up On The Roof.

1: The Seeds Are Sown

Robson Green grew up within a few miles of this view of the goose-neck cranes from the Tyneside shipyards looking towards Newcastle. This is the gateway to the north-east, the home of the Geordie and of a football team that has, until recently, lived in the shadow of its glorious past. There is an historic link between Robson's beloved north-eastern homeland and Jerome Flynn's more insulated south-east, although it occurred long before either of them were born. In the desperate years of the 1930s when morale in the Tyneside mining community was at its lowest ebb, the people of Sevenoaks in Kent "adopted" a mining village sending both money and food parcels until there were signs of improvement. Robson's forebears were miners, Jerome's home town is Sevenoaks. The friendship between south and north is reflected today in a partnership which is delighting millions.

Jerome grew up at Ide Hill, a small village near Sevenoaks in Kent gloriously placed on the greensand ridge high above the Weald of Kent. The spire of the church and the clock in its tower have the distinction of being the highest in Kent. Jerome was christened in this church and attended the local primary school (just out of the picture). In later years he took part in tug o' war contests on this village green and, in 1995, after the release of Unchained Melody and White Cliffs, officially opened the Spring Bank Holiday fair. On that occasion, however, he was mobbed by hundreds of fans.

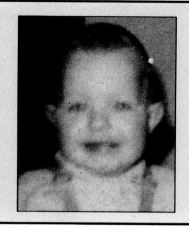

ROBSON GOLIGHTLY GREEN

BORN: DECEMBER 18TH, 1964
at **DILSTON HOSPITAL,
HEXHAM, NORTHUMBERLAND**

WEIGHT: 7lbs 3 oz.

**FIRST SON TO ROBSON
AND ANNE GREEN: A BROTHER
FOR DAWN AND JOANNA**

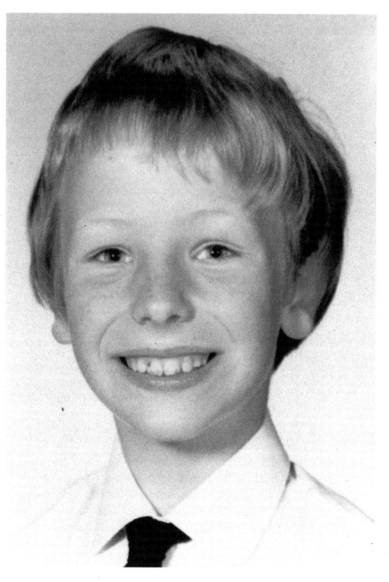

Robson Golightly Green as a confident schoolboy at the age of six at home in the north-east mining village of Dudley. His father is also called Robson, the fourth-generation of mining stock, a man fiercely proud of his roots and, as a Geordie, the possessor of a wonderful accent, almost impenetrable to a southerner. His mother is Anne, chatty, good natured, vivacious with a strong sense of identity that is so special among Tynesiders. A north-east mining tradition, reserved for the eldest son, is for him to be given names made out of earlier well-established family names. Robson, a famous appellation in Tyneside, was his grandmother's surname and Golightly, his great uncle's surname. Mr Golightly, who died when his ship was torpedoed in 1944, was a union leader and controversially involved in the coal dispute of 1926 which led to the Great Strike.

JEROME PATRICK FLYNN

BORN: MARCH 16th, 1963
at FARNBOROUGH HOSPITAL,
BROMLEY, KENT

WEIGHT: 9 lbs

SECOND SON FOR ERIC AND
FERN FLYNN: A BROTHER
FOR KERRY AND DANIEL

Jerome with his father Eric, actor by profession and village cricketer on a Sunday afternoon. In July 1963, some four months after Jerome was born Eric, or Paddy as he was better known, was playing at Chaldon in Surrey. He hit a six and the ball rebounded off the handle of the pram, just inches from Jerome's head. Eric remembers the incident well. He retired from the match and spent the rest of the afternoon being sick. "It was Jerome's first cricket season", he said, "and almost his last".

The new baby was nearly called Patrick but the thought of two "Paddys" in one family was altogether too confusing. Then he was to have been Joseph but eventually Jerome seemed more suitable.

Although Robson and Jerome were born 21 months and almost 300 miles apart, they were children of the sixties, and music was to be an important part of their lives. Jerome came into the world during the time when a fever known as Beatlemania was sweeping across much of England. The Fab Four had just released two new records, She Loves You and From Me To You and were well on course to become demi-gods to an entire generation.

Jerome's father Eric played the guitar and was an accomplished singer. Photograph shows him playing the lead in the first London production of Company, by Stephen Sondheim, in 1972.

Robson senior was also a singer and a great Elvis Presley fan. After five days in the pits, often at the coal face, he enjoyed the fellowship which Dudley Working Men's Club provided on a Saturday night where he spoke enthusiastically about the size of his leeks, the speed of his racing pigeons and, when in the mood, dressed up in his Teddy Boy gear and sang a few well-known numbers. His favourite song in 1964 was called I Believe, recorded by The Bachelors, which had been in the charts for 17 weeks that year, reaching number two behind The Beatles' Can't Buy Me Love.

Photograph shows Robson senior in 1968 on his way to winning a singing competition.

Robson on holiday with mum and younger brother David. Anne Green remembers how Robson loved showing off and was always happy, cheerful and mischievous. When David was born and the focus of attention switched to the little fellow lying on the floor kicking his legs in the air, Robson mounted his toy tractor and, with his legs furiously pumping at the pedals, worked up enough head of steam to take him straight over the body of the bewildered baby. Robson always remembers that incident for he reversed even quicker to avoid his punishment.

*Jerome aged five with his brother Daniel, six, in their grandparents'
garden near Sevenoaks. Jerome was a sensitive and kind boy, with a firm
sense of fair play, but once, at a very early age, while pretending to be
Captain Hook, threw a knife at his brother with great force. His sister
Kerry shouted "duck". Daniel, too young to know what the word meant,
nevertheless did so instinctively. The knife embedded itself in the kitchen
door just above his head.*

LIKE all boys growing up in the country Robson and Jerome had their own special adventure playgrounds. Robson's kingdom was the banks of a small rocky burn that ran from the back of his house in Wansbeck Road, Dudley across the moors to two huge lakes. The line of semi-detached houses stopped at the river and once the low wall had been scaled and the seven foot drop carefully negotiated, the land beyond provided an abundance of pleasures. On one occasion, however, Robson missed his footing, fell head first into the rocky waters and knocked himself out. He was taken by ambulance to the Royal Victoria Infirmary at Newcastle where he quickly recovered.

Jerome liked climbing and would scale anything from a 30ft cherry tree in the garden to the roof of the family bungalow. He was an adventurer and, over a period of time in his pre-school years, spurred on by his older brother or sister, he managed to start a fire in the garage, fill the mini-van with water, break some newly-delivered tiles with the unerring aim of a future bowler and jump into his grandparents' swimming pool, before he had learned to swim. His mother, fully clothed, had to dive in to rescue him.

Jerome on holiday in Tintagel, Cornwall with mum, Fern, sister Kerry and brother Daniel. With three small children Fern was coming to terms with the fact that her acting career was in suspense. She had trained at the Royal Academy of Dramatic Art where she won the Shakespeare Scholarship and met her husband, but had barely started on her career before the arrival of the children in quick succession. She finally abandoned the stage in 1968, finding the demands of a theatrical career incompatible with raising a family.

Robson's first school was Dudley Primary and his first school play was Joseph and the Amazing Technicolour Dreamcoat. He was chosen for the title role but that didn't please him because he thought that Joseph was a wimp. He wanted to play the Pharaoh who had an Elvis number to sing and got the best laughs. However, he settled for Joseph and gave what his teacher Mrs Anderson described as a "commanding performance."

ROBSON's greatest passion was football. On one occasion he was picked for his school team, took his place on the right wing and so missed a vital rehearsal for the school production of *Peter Pan* in which he was due to play Captain Hook At that stage in his life acting took second place.

School football was fun but it was nothing compared to the regular Saturday afternoon trip to St James' Park, the home of Newcastle United. Robson would watch the Magpies with his brother and father, all of them longing for the side to show some consistency. But the real glory days belonged to the past. Oh for another Jackie Milburn, Jimmy Scoular or Hughie Gallacher! Oh for a good cup run! On occasions the future of Newcastle United seemed as bleak as a grey day in Seaton Burn Colliery.

Jerome also played football and supported Tottenham Hotspur but, encouraged by his father, his greatest love was cricket. Before he was big enough to earn a place in the village side, Jerome played for Ide Hill juniors, a team managed, on occasions, by his mother.

Picture above shows Jerome's maternal grandfather Richard Warner, or 'Grandick', with whom Jerome had a special relationship. Richard, of stage screen and television, was an actor rarely out of work. Right is Robson's 'best friend', Grandad Matheson Green a former miner seen here with one of Robson senior's chasers which he bought with his redundancy money from the mines some years before. Matheson's love for horses stems from his days in the horse infantry during the 1914-18 war. During the second world war both Matheson Green and Richard Warner were 'desert rats' — the nickname used for soldiers who served with the British 7th Armoured Division in the North African campaign of 1941-42.

ONE of the most memorable moments in Robson's early life was the day he met his greatest hero, Malcolm MacDonald. In 1973 'Supermac' as he was known was invited to open a launderette opposite Dudley School. Having made a small speech and cut the tape he was asked if he could spare a few moments to chat to the children during their dinner break. There were 400 in the school hall and nine at each table but to Robson's delight the great man pulled up a chair, sat between him and Colin Hudson and chatted to them about the three goals he had scored against Liverpool on his debut for Newcastle and of his own great wish to win a cup-winner's medal. Robson was his number one fan and devastated when 'Supermac' was transferred to Arsenal.

Jerome never met his hero. But he followed the deeds of the larger-than-life Ian Botham with great interest, playing his own cricket — albeit at village standard — in the same attacking vein. In his first match for the Ide Hill senior team when he was 12 his father, Eric, bet him 50p he couldn't hit a six. Jerome smashed the first ball he received over the pavilion and later claimed his prize.

As he grew older Jerome became an accomplished striker of the ball and a fast bowler and he regularly picked up the prizes for hitting the most sixes or taking the most wickets for Ide Hill. He also turned out for the local side while on holiday in Pembrokeshire, scoring on one occasion a 'Beefy' type century and then concussing one of the locals with a viciously fast delivery.

Malcolm MacDonald who was known in Newcastle and throughout the football world as 'Supermac'. He first played for Knole Juniors in Jerome's home town of Sevenoaks before moving to Newcastle via Tonbridge and Fulham.

Pembrokeshire — the beautiful county of the south-west extremity of Wales where Jerome formed a strong bond with the Welsh-speaking locals, enjoyed walking the coastal path and surfing when the waves were high.

2: The Young Entertainers

WHEN Robson was 11 he graduated to Seaton Burn High School and new interests entered his life. He bought a secondhand acoustic guitar and practised until his fingers were sore. He joined the Air Training Corps and enjoyed fishing and rafting on the burn. A vast building site at Dudley made a wonderful playground for Robson and his mates and when the men had packed up for the weekend the boys would store planks of wood in a garage and then make their own rafts. The burn led to a huge lake, full of fish.

In 1977 Robson and his friend Keith Hudson auditioned for the annual Miners' Gala Competition and were delighted to be invited to take part. They decided to sing the Laurel and Hardy number, *The Blue Ridge Mountains of Virginia* and, for a special laugh, Keith was going to copy Oliver Hardy and pretend to knock his mate over with a rolling pin when they got to the high notes. "Unfortunately", said Robson, "he struck too hard, knocked me out and our act was cancelled".

Robson's desire to entertain, especially on stage, led him to the Backworth Drama Centre where the resident director was Max Roberts. Once a week in the evening, he would catch a bus to Backworth and meet his friend, Joe Caffrey, another would-be actor from Newcastle. The boys enjoyed the plays and the readings and occasional trips to perform in local schools. Robson remembers reading scripts by such talented writers as Alan Plater, Cecil Taylor, Tom Hadaway and Michael Chaplin and began to think in terms of acting as a career possibility should he not be able to pursue his then burning desire to be a pilot in the RAF. He was 15.

Another great catch for Robson and David on a caravan holiday.

JEROME moved from Ide Hill School, to Solefields, a preparatory school, where he took part in his first school play *The Mikado*, playing Katisha, a jealous older woman. From there he went to Wildernesse Secondary where he enjoyed football, rugby and especially the competitiveness of cricket, passionately enjoying the battle between batsman and bowler. But his life took a most unexpected turn when he was 15 and his brother Daniel asked him if he would like a part in the Sevenoaks Youth Theatre's production of *The Crucible*. Daniel was the director, one of the cast had dropped out and he needed to fill the leading part of John Proctor. Jerome, after some hesitation, accepted the offer.

His father, Eric, remembers the performance and the intensity of the scenes and Jerome's contemporaries were impressed by his charisma and stage presence. As far as Jerome was concerned he was hooked. The feeling of having to sustain a character in front of an audience for two hours on stage and take them with him on a journey, such as John Proctor took, was hugely exciting. At last he had found something that he was good at apart from sport, which earned him the respect of his peers and friends. "Arthur Miller's writing was so powerful", said Jerome, "that I would come off stage completely overwhelmed. Suddenly girls seemed to be more interested in me and that was a very good reason to carry on. *The Crucible* got me thinking seriously about acting as a career. *Charley's Aunt*, a school production which followed, cemented it."

Robson and Jerome loved sport and participated enthusiastically. Robson played football, hockey and was a great angler. Jerome played football, rugby and excelled at cricket. In 1978 he caught the eye of the Kent scouts searching the county for talent and was invited to play in an Under-16 match against Essex on the Neville ground at Tunbridge Wells. Jerome batted for only 13 overs but in that time scored 112 runs — his maiden hundred. His father, Eric, desperate to watch the match, arrived in time to see the first of Jerome's dozen sixes — having completed his own century. He was clocked by the police doing 115 miles an hour on the motorway and given a speeding ticket!

*Jerome in the Wildernesse School production of Charley's Aunt. He went
to the school in Sevenoaks after failing his 11-plus. "I actually took the
exam without knowing it", he said, "but I think it was a good move for me
to go to a secondary modern school which had excellent teachers but a
few rough pupils. It prepared me for a more realistic view of life.
Certainly I became intensely competitive, particularly in sport".
According to his teacher, Mike Evans, that also applied to his approach to
drama and his performance in Charley's Aunt was triumphantly funny.*

Robson was also 15 when Seaton Burn High drama society entrusted him with a starring role in The Pirates of Penzance. He didn't let them down and, according to a former teacher, was a "wow" with the girls. More musicals followed and Robson, already determined that he would not follow his father and grandfather into the mines, wondered if there might be a place for him one day in the perilous world of show business.
It was either that or the Royal Air Force.

IN 1979 Jerome was "auditioned" for the job as lead singer with *System X,* a band which had been formed by his brother's public school friends. "I think they were desperate", said Jerome, "and as I was the only one who auditioned they gave me the job". The first gig took place at Sevenoaks School and, after the performance was over, there was a fight between Jerome's mates from Wildernesse Secondary and the public schoolboys of Sevenoaks. "I was very confused", said Jerome. "I did not know who to fight, so I watched them whacking each other."

The second and last gig for *System X* took place at the annual Ide Hill cricket club dance and, as Jerome began to sing the Stranglers' song *No More Heroes* his cronies started to boo. "I realised the music was not quite what the organisers had in mind. It was too punk rock for them. I remember how the boos completely drowned the vocals. They gave me a hell of a time but it was all in good fun really."

Robson also had a small group called *Solid State* and his school chums were entertained to eight-minute gigs during the lunch break. By now he had bought a new electric guitar and practised every night in his bedroom. The first tune he perfected was called *Hang Down Your Head, Tom Dooley.* It sounded great, especially when he switched on his five-watt amplifier but David, always ready with a schoolboy observation about his elder brother's guitar playing, said he could fart louder!

Robson continued strumming and developed a bigger repertoire, mainly of old rock 'n roll tunes — miraculously without disturbing the neighbours. Next door his mate Geoffrey Beadling was in a colliery band and played the trumpet. He, too, practised in the bedroom drowning out the sounds of Robson and his guitar.

Robson learned to play the double bass with a modicum of success. He also tried the violin but gave up.

As a teenager and for many years to follow Jerome had lots of girl friends. "I was very passionate as a child", he said, "and it was not just about cricket and competition and friends, but also about love. I confess to being a hopeless romantic, until quite recently. I was in love with the feeling of being in love and when that feeling started to fade I would get terrified and run a mile. I was convinced that true happiness lay in finding the perfect girl and perfect meant I had to feel totally dreamy and fantastic all the time just like in the films. When it came to love I was, without doubt, an irresponsible young man." Certainly Jerome had his leg pulled frequently by his maternal grandfather, Grandick, who would often say: "Well Jerome, who are we in love with this week!"

Robson was a keen member of the Air Training Corps at Seaton Burn. He arranged gigs for them and acted as DJ. He went on camp, visited RAF stations, took gliding lessons at RAF Leeming and spent an exciting week in Cyprus where he devoted much of his spare time to entertaining his mates with songs, stories and his newly acquired ability to impersonate well-known characters. On one holiday in Austria he had his friends in stitches all week with his impression of the voices and characteristics of teachers, especially the headmaster Mr White. The leader of the school group was both impressed and amused by Robson's ability to parody and capture, so accurately, the personality of his "victim". Robson once organised the boarding of a school coach by calling out the names using the headmaster's voice.

THERE had been many small coincidences in the early years to link Robson and Jerome despite their contrasting backgrounds. Both were on holiday with their families when their hero Elvis Presley — the king of rock 'n roll — died. Robson's great footballing hero, Malcolm MacDonald played as a junior in Jerome's home town of Sevenoaks. Their respective grandads were 'desert rats'. Now there were to be two more. Jerome's first LP, which he played over and over again, was called *Twenty Five Rockin' and Rollin' Greats*. It was also Robson's first LP, and he loved it. Remarkably they also shared the same favourite film — *It's a Wonderful Life*, starring James Stewart.

Robson, in fact, was a great cinema-goer and would also watch the old black and white movies on television whenever he could. "I loved people who spoke, wrote and sang from their hearts", he said. "actors like Spencer Tracey, Jimmy Stewart and Marlon Brando; writers like George Orwell, Tom Sharpe and Sid Chaplin; singers like Elvis, Sam Cooke, Little Richard and the late Otis Redding."

The largest musical influence on Jerome's early life was The Beatles. He said: "My parents' record collection was extremely small but they had all The Beatles records and my brother, sister and I would spend hours singing their songs and learning their harmonies. Lennon and McCartney were my heroes". His favourite singers also included Elvis, Ella Fitzgerald, Sam Cooke, The Drifters and Frank Sinatra. Other influential figures were Arthur Miller (for his writing), James Stewart (for his acting) and Jerry Lewis (for his comedy) but, probably most of all, Natalie Wood who he first saw in *West Side Story* and with whom he became completely besotted.

There was another early link between Robson and Jerome and that was their ability to impersonate well-known characters. Jerome's favourite was Tommy Cooper while Robson adored Stan Laurel, the slapstick comedian whose adventures with Oliver Hardy were cinema classics. On some of his school trips Robson shared a room with Andy Sinton who would occasionally say: "I'm depressed Robbo. Do your Stan Laurel". Andy and Robson played football together, but only briefly because Andy went on to play for England Schoolboys, Queen's Park Rangers, Spurs and England.

A big moment in Jerome's life was the day his parents moved. "We never had much money but we were able to get a lovely piece of land very cheaply. The house was a bit of a wreck so we had to pull together and make it habitable. We grew our own vegetables and split 120 logs a week for our wood-burning stove. It was hard work but greatly rewarding as it brought us closer to each other and to nature".

Stan Laurel, the slapstick comedian whom Robson liked to impersonate. In his films with Oliver Hardy, Laurel's misunderstanding of certain lines led to ever-escalating chaos. He was also, indirectly, responsible for Robson failing his O-level drama exam! "In the oral test", Robson said "I played Orsino in Shakespeare's Twelfth Night and, in order to give the character more zest and fun, decided to base him on Stan Laurel. I practised the part to perfection and on the vital day faced the examiners with great confidence. 'Oh spirit of love, how quick and fresh art thou'...and with that fell flat on my face, just like Stan Laurel would have done. Some weeks later I heard that I had failed my drama O-level. I was told it was rubbish, and I suppose that it was. They advised me not to try acting as a career. I was despondent."

Tommy Cooper, the late and much-loved comedian and conjurer who wore a red fez and told hilarious stories. Cooper, who had his own TV show for many years, is one of Jerome's favourite characters. On many social occasions, to the delight of his friends, a shambling figure with a crooked nose and a red fez would appear from nowhere, tell several jokes and finish with the well-known catchphrase "just like that". One such appearance was at brother Dan's wedding.

ROBSON left Seaton Burn High at the age of 17 having already decided that a career in the RAF was not a reality for one who had an aversion to military discipline. Instead he signed on as an apprentice draughtsman at Swan Hunter and, for the experience, spent the first few months of his working life as a welder, a burner and a shipwright. Every morning he would leave home at Dudley and cycle the six miles to Wallsend Shipyard. As he welded he thought of fishing and football at St James' Park. But most of all he thought of the theatre and the stage and his burning desire to entertain.

His mother Anne remembers how Robson was always surrounded by friends. Before he left school and found a flat of his own he would ask plaintively: "Mum, can I have a few friends around tonight?". She always agreed, knowing that seven or eight would turn up for a jam session. They listened to pop music getting great pleasure from one particular group, *The Flying Pickets*, who harmonised, without accompaniment and shot into the pop charts. In 1984 Robson, with three other boys and four girls decided to adopt their style and formed an A Capella group which they called, *The Worky Tickets*.

The Worky Tickets were a great successs, entertaining old and young, enjoying local gigs and earning an invitation from Tyne Tees Television to appear in one of their regional magazine programmes called *The Works*. Robson dyed his hair red for the occasion and was the only one who liked the colour. They sang *The Wanderer* and the publicity led to more bookings for *The Worky Tickets* including a request to sing at the Albert Hall in London.

Jerome also left school with no plans of higher education other than possibly following his brother into the Royal Academy for Dramatic Art (RADA). First, however, he needed to earn money and so joined the team of construction workers building the M25 about two miles north of his house and quickly became the butt of some practical joking that amused everyone except Jerome. On one occasion he was told to use his strength to bend some iron bars into a particular shape. Jerome, ever willing, complied with his instructions and spent one day on the hard shoulder of this unfinished motorway completing the task. After eight hours he was totally exhausted. Imagine his surprise when he saw the same job being efficiently tackled by a hydraulic machine in three seconds flat. Nearby the gang were laughing mercilessly!

The misery of the motorway continued. Having nearly killed the overseer by driving a JCB down a bank, he was mighty glad to get the sack when the same man found him in a nearby pub during working hours. Jerome had rushed into the inn to warn the workers, mainly Irishmen, that the boss was on his way. They thanked him, thrust a pint in his hand and shot out of the back door as the governor walked into the public bar.

Robson with his brother and sister, David and Joanna. Although he had left home Robson regularly came back to meet them, his mum and dad, grandad and grandma and elder sister Dawn. "They lived within five miles of each other", he said. "It gave me some sort of identity."

1984 was the year of the miners' strike. In Dudley and Seaton Burn and right across the north-east there were angry rallies, bitter confrontations and the most amazing loyalties, all sparked off by Arthur Scargill's (correct) suspicion that the Government planned to close half the country's pits. The show of solidarity in the north-east would not work without financial help and among the many fund-raising events was a concert at the Albert Hall in March of that year. Robson's Worky Tickets were on the bill. They are seen here in rehearsal. Among those who sang with Robson (second from left) were: Libby Davison, Joe Caffrey, Ali Burridge, Dean Marriner, Gill Burridge, Paula Holland, Stuart Turnbull, Shelley and Hufty. They sang A Cappella — in the style of the chapel. A worky ticket is someone who makes a nuisance of himself.

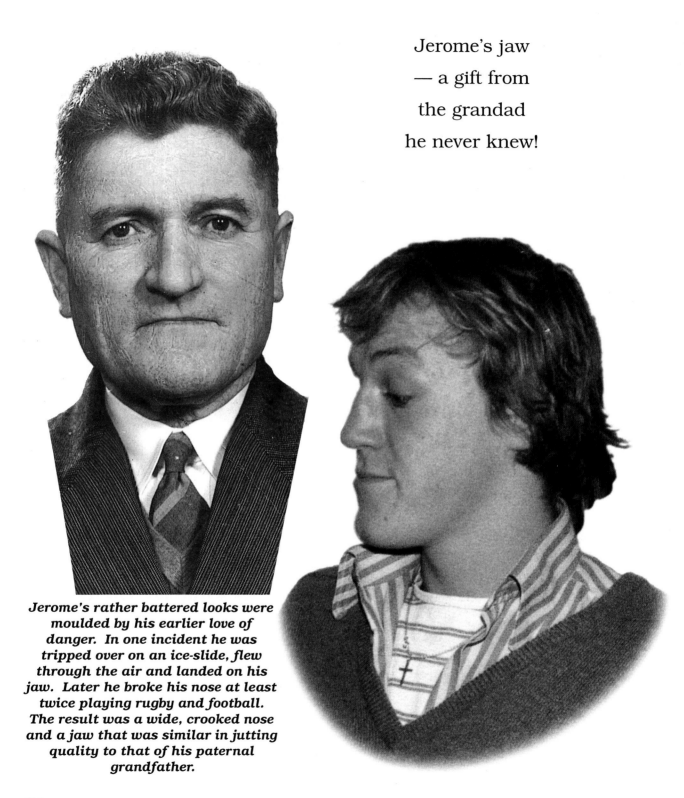

Jerome's jaw
— a gift from
the grandad
he never knew!

Jerome's rather battered looks were moulded by his earlier love of danger. In one incident he was tripped over on an ice-slide, flew through the air and landed on his jaw. Later he broke his nose at least twice playing rugby and football. The result was a wide, crooked nose and a jaw that was similar in jutting quality to that of his paternal grandfather.

3: Drama School And Live Theatre

ERIC Flynn was on a theatrical tour of South Africa in the autumn of 1980 and, by flying out to join him, Jerome missed an audition with RADA. On his return, however, he applied for a place at the Central School for Speech and Drama and proved to them he had the right qualities to train as an actor.

He enjoyed drama school but found it so difficult to live on £2 a week that he made his home, with friends, in a London squat (originally founded by Paul McGann). Jerome enjoyed a hectic social life but, true to form, met with one or two misadventures on the way. On one occasion he and Steve O'Donnell climbed a tree at Swiss Cottage and, from a height of about 40 feet, Jerome missed his footing and plunged earthwards. His fall was broken by branches but, as he hit the ground, he managed a forward roll — a trick perfected during his earlier years in the rhododendrons of Kent. Although he was no longer in the countryside he could not stop climbing trees, and occasionally builders' scaffolding, which was Jerome's way of sitting "on top of the world". "I enjoyed working and living in London", he said. "It was an opportunity to meet people from other cultures — a time of discovery — but my passion for climbing did not diminish."

One of his friends at Central was Amanda Royle, a vegan. "When I sat next to her with a piece of meat", Jerome said, "she used to give me an earful." After a friendly lecture about the obscenities that are carried out on animals in getting them ready for human consumption, he asked her to produce some evidence of this, which she did. Impressed by Amanda's ability to abstain from eating flesh, fish and fowl and alerted to modern factory farming methods, Jerome felt compelled to adopt a diet of vegetables, cereals, seeds and fruit. After a while he amended this to include fish and dairy products but from that moment he became a non-carnivore.

Robson, meanwhile, was qualifying as a draughtsman at Swan Hunter, the massive Tyneside shipbuilders. During his apprenticeship he made rapid progress, helping to design the hull for the new *Ark Royal* and the *Coventry* but he hated the rigidity of the work and the nine-to-five routine. "The clock in the design office", he said, "was the slowest in Britain. Every day seemed like an eternity and I soon realised that if British shipbuilding and me were to survive we would have to part company". Robson shocked his bosses and his father by quitting the job and, thanks to his great friend Max Roberts who had moved from Backworth Drama Centre, he joined Live Theatre, a semi-professional company of actors with a small theatre near the Quayside, Newcastle.

His father was alarmed by Robson's decision to leave. "In the north-east", he said, "with the years of depression, the unemployment and the hunger still a vivid nightmare and with the uncertainty that existed over the future of the collieries, a man with a good job in a shipyard was very lucky. And Robson, a skilled draughtsman, decided to leave. I wouldn't have been so concerned if he'd wanted to be a professional footballer or darts player — but an ACTOR. I thought he was mad."

B Y now Robson lived in a flat at Heaton which he shared with two lads, Ronnie Johnson and 'Scouse' George Hatton. The flat was called "The Bermuda Triangle" because there were so many parties that when a friend went in, it was a long time before he came out again! On Sundays Robson always returned home to Dudley to see his mam, usually with a pile of washing and a good appetite. Anne Green had not shared her ex-husband's concern over her son's big gamble in exchanging the security of Swan Hunter for the precarious Live Theatre. But then she was never certain exactly what he was doing except that he bounded in the front door full of energy and enthusiasm, talked non-stop and then disappeared as soon as he had devoured his Sunday lunch.

The admirable Max Roberts was a name that always cropped up in conversation and so was the charismatic Tom Hadaway, a good friend from Whitley Bay who was a story teller and playwright. Tom had achieved considerable fame with his play *The Long Line* and national renown with his contribution to the Geordie series *When the Boat Comes In.* His enthusiasm for Live Theatre was legion and his respect for Robson, the actor, clearly shown by his constant encouragement.

Robson enjoyed his days of touring. With such actors as Alan Plater, Tim Healey and Alan Armstrong he visited Kendal, Rhyll, Skegness, Bognor, Doncaster and Edinburgh. They also played in welfare halls all around Tyneside and earned a reputation as one of the best small professional companies in the north-east. "Live Theatre was a valuable outlet for writers", said Robson "and it was a company that gave a chance to talented actors from Tyneside." One of his favourite plays was called *Come Snow, Come Blow,* performed in 1987. Robson played the part of Atwood Ruddy, a misguided buffoon who dreamed of winning the Morpeth to Newcastle Road Race but had been disqualified in previous years for catching the bus. It was a surreal comedy by Leonard Barras and to this day Robson considers Ruddy to be his favourite character portrayal.

With such successes Robson thought it was a good time to apply for the valuable actor's union card from the local branch of Equity and was somewhat dismayed to see it awarded to four strippers while his application was refused. He tried again. This time he was successful and immediately persuaded the Tyne Opera House that he could sing like a nightingale. However Robson was totally unprepared and during rehearsals for a forthcoming opera he was seen to be miming while the rest of the cast were trilling merrily. Invited then to sing on his own Robson was gently told to come back when he had learned the words and the tune. His confidence had taken a bit of a battering so he applied instead for a straight part in *The Hunchback of Notre Dame.* "Can you handle a sword?",

he was asked. "Perfectly well", he an-
swered, determined to take lessons the
moment he returned to Newcastle. To
his great dismay a sword was then produced. His bluff had been called again.

Robson continued with *Live Theatre. Hands*, 1986, *Kiddars Luck*, 1988,
In Blackberry Time, 1988. "The characters I portrayed always came from
the north-east", said Robson. "Tyneside
in particular contains a gallery of fantastic people whose ability to survive
adversity stems from their struggles of
the past. My home is the north-east
and always will be."

Live Theatre taps rich vein of talents

The Long Line, at the Live
Theatre, Newcastle, until
July 26.

SOMEWHERE in
England it is possible
there is a small-scale
theatre company capable
drawing on the sort of
·urces assembled in
·oduction.
·e it is possible
contained in a
·n the sort of
'rit which

birth to this company and
some who have since
enriched its history, returning pugnaciously to ensure
that the new venue is
launched in style and with
impact.

David Whitaker, Val
McLane, Anne Orwin, Sammy
Johnson and Denise Bryson
are joined by young Robson
Green, to whom I can pay no
finer compliment than to say
he looks fully at home in
their company.

Hadaway's play, typically
·inged by a ·

cations.
What Max Roberts's pro-
duction has done is to
recover the reputation which
this once fine company had
begun to lose in the last
couple of years.

What the commitment of a
fine writer and some first-
rate actors (plus a little new
blood) has done is to reju-
venate Live Theatre as
crucial moment in its
short but sometimes
dynamic history.

Yes, of cours·
look a little ·
more re·

*Robson's first 'theatrical'
photograph and (top left) the Live
Theatre at Newcastle. Here, his
credits included The Long Line,
Scrap, and Your Home in the
West. He also performed at the
Tyne Theatre and with the
Northern Stage Company.*

CENTRAL did not have to look far to find the most suitable student to play the title role of *Huckleberry Finn* in an adaptation of Mark Twain's classic book. Jerome Flynn was not only similar in name but his outlook on life matched that of the young voyager, dressed in clothes that had seen better days, who sailed in a raft down the Mississippi and whistled and sang his way through a series of stirring adventures. Huck Finn was so at home with nature that the book could have been written with Jerome Flynn in mind.

This was his first lead in his final year at Central and he followed it up with another good performance in *Flying Blind*. But while Jerome was impressing theatrical agents in London, Robson was wowing the critics in Newcastle, particularly with his performance in Tom Hadaway's *The Long Line* — a play that fitted in perfectly with Robson's own tough, north-east background

The Long Line traced the fluctuating fortunes of a North Shields fishing family through more than 100 years. Robson had several roles to play and earned this appreciation from the *Newcastle Journal*. ***"I'd single out young Robson Green as an example of restrained but convincing acting that would be hard to beat anywhere....Even when playing the minor role of a clerk he gives the assignment a few touches which lift the man off the page and into three dimensions. When he's playing George Pearson, the skinhead dropout in part three, you can't take your eyes off this marvellously inventive actor".***

There was someone more important than the critics sitting in the audience on that opening night. Robson Green senior was there, enthralled by his son's awesome portrayal of George Pearson, totally converted to the idea that he might be an actor after all and delighted by the press notice which read "Green For Go".

These were happy and exciting days for the ambitious Robson who now yearned for greater things. For the less ambitious Jerome, however, life drifted sweetly along. He enjoyed singing with Carte Blanche and, in particular, a duet with his great friend Steve O'Donnell — their favourite number being the Nat King Cole/Dean Martin song, *Long Long Ago*. Jerome said: "On one occasion we were performing at the New End Theatre, Hampstead and there were nine of us on stage and two in the audience. But that didn't matter. I'd never been happier. I was dressed up in a dinner suit singing in harmony with my mates, re-living my old fantasies about appearing in MGM musicals and comedy dramas with the likes of Dean Martin and Jerry Lewis, Frank Sinatra and Bing Crosby. These were very special days".

Jerome sang with a group who called themselves Carte Blanche. During his last year at Central School for Speech and Drama, Jerome readily agreed to join seven other actors and sing a number of well-known, nostalgic, mainly American show numbers. Carte Blanche put on a concert at Central and then toured the clubs including Maxim's de Paris. This decision to perform outside of drama school was a wise one — the four boys and four girls individually qualified as members of the British Actors' Equity Association. This enabled them to apply for the essential trade union card which was hard to come by in those days. Left to right Jerome, Serena Evans, (future sister-in law), Bill Osborn, Nancy Gair, Bill Champion, Amanda Royle, Steve O'Donnell, Nancy Crane.

Robson as George Pearson in Tom Hadaway's The Long Line.

Jerome as Huck Finn at the Central School for Speech and Drama.

JEROME left Central, found himself an agent and almost immediately had to put on uniform as a soldier in the controversial BBC drama serial, *The Monocled Mutineer* which highlighted atrocities inside the British Army during the 1914-18 war. Jerome played hard-man Frannie, a member of actor Paul McGann's rebellious gang. The serial was filmed in Aberdovey where Paul and Jerome shared a flat and struck up a great friendship. Jerome then made his theatrical debut at Manchester's Contact Theatre in *Firestone* and later played at The Royal Court in London as a gin player in David Mammett's *Prairie Du Chien*. He landed the part of Freddie in Euston Films' *The Fear* playing a jowly, likeable henchman to Ian Glenn who was also to become a close friend. The jobs kept coming. After playing Nigel in the BBC Screen On Two, germ-warfare drama, *The Russian Soldier,* Jerome moved on to the big screen playing Joe in *A Summer Story.*

Then came Jerome's big break into popular TV — an invitation to play the part of another lovable tough guy called Rambo in Jack Rosenthal's pilot television film, *London's Burning.* The film was a triumph and all the cast signed on for the series which was set to follow — all, that is, except Jerome. "It was too early for me to get trapped in a series," he said. "I was just two years out of drama school and my career wasn't firmly established, besides which the character didn't really excite me."

So Jerome left *London's Burning* causing some consternation among the production staff by so doing. His decision was vindicated when he was offered a season with the Royal Shakespeare Company. At Stratford he played Orlando in *As You Like It* with Sophie Thompson and went with the play to Newcastle unaware that an important part of his future, a certain Robson Green, would be in the audience for one of the performances.

Robson, in fact, had also made the break into peak-hour television when he successfully auditioned for the BBC Screen One production *A Night on The Tyne.* He then went up for a part in the fourth series of *Casualty,* already well established and highly popular. The casting directors wanted a young man to play Jimmy the Geordie hospital porter. To the delight of his friends in the north, Robson got the job and at last he was on his way.

For three "wonderful series" Robson played Jimmy, achieving national recognition for his gritty, down-to-earth but humorous portrayal of the comic porter. He now wanted a more significant role and wondered if he could possibly be one of the first porters in medical history to graduate as a nurse or even a doctor! While he was considering his move there came an opportunity he couldn't miss. Central TV was looking for someone to play the part of a lazy, good-for-nothing Geordie soldier who would always be in trouble for dressing scruffily or being late on parade or misunderstanding simple instructions. The character was to be called Fusilier

Dave Tucker and the film was a pilot for a possible series to be called *Soldier, Soldier*, scheduled to be screened in January 1991.

Robson remembers that first audition: "There were five on the panel sitting in a row and I walked through the door and straight past them, pretending there was no-one there. They were looking for a clown so I acted like one, eventually going down on one knee and pleading — 'give me the job, I need the money'. Finally, after four auditions, Zelda Barron, the director, said they were casting me for the part. I 'phoned Alison, with the news and told her I was coming home to celebrate. Between York and Northallerton the train broke down and remained in the sidings for more than eight hours. So I toasted Fusilier Tucker on my own — with British Rail Côte du Rhone!"

Robson with his mum and dad after his wedding to Alison Ogilvie, the young lady he met at Manchester while she was training to be an occupational therapist. The service was at Alison's home town of Ashington on June 22nd, 1991. The guests included actors, directors, writers, shipbuilders, footballers and, of course, his family. "In fact", said Robson, "everyone I loved was there."

Robson in "Hands", BBC TV 1986.

Jerome in "London's Burning". Too early to be trapped in a series.

ROBSON Green had never heard of Jerome Flynn but he was impressed by his Orlando at the Theatre Royal Newcastle and wondered if their paths would ever cross. Little did he know that Jerome was regularly driving to the Northumberland fishing village of Amble and, on the way, passing very close to Robson's own home.

Jerome, in fact, was on a mission to see a new friend — Freddie the Dolphin, who lived in the North Sea. It had been his lifelong ambition to swim with a dolphin, an ambition he never expected to realise and he certainly had no idea that one was living off the English coast. Jerome said: "Steve Waddington, who was appearing with me in *As You Like It,* told me about Freddie, so we drove to Amble, stayed the night in the village and turned up at the quay the next morning, only to find the sea was too rough. So we went to the nearby pub and chatted to the locals until the weather improved. After about two hours Gordon the boatman appeared and said: 'Come on, let's go'."

"We put on our wet suits, got into the boat and sailed to the end of the harbour. Suddenly this huge animal appeared and leapt 10 feet out of the water in an arc. Steve and I screamed with delight and I can honestly say that moment changed my view of life. As I swam with Freddie I realised he was urging me to let go of whatever I was holding on to in my mind. There he was, a highly intelligent, hugely powerful wild animal, weighing a quarter of a ton, swimming alongside and skimming me as he jumped out and then splashed back into the sea. He could have killed me but I felt completely safe. I think he was sharing with me the joy of simply being alive. He was directly challenging me to express the life within me, rather than stay trapped in my own personal life."

Jerome bought a wet suit, returned every weekend to meet Freddie, usually with friends from the company and was rather disappointed when the time came to leave. He returned south and later played Alcibiades in the "hugely enjoyable" *Timon of Athens* at the Young Vic— a character and a production he then regarded as one of the best he had been involved with. He appeared in Birmingham in *Who's Afraid of Virginia Woolf* with Sylvia Sims, her daughter Beattie Edney and James Bolam and then took time off to widen his horizons. Jerome spent three months in Thailand with friends and was delighted with this opportunity to experience other people's cultures.

During another break from acting he renewed his affinity with dolphins, this time with a famous fellow called Fungi from Dingle Bay, County Kerry on the west coast of Ireland. The trip was made particularly special for Jerome when he persuaded his greatest friend, brother Dan, to join him on the adventure. It was not only an opportunity for them to swim with a wild dolphin but to visit their Celtic roots together for the first time — their paternal grandfather George had been one of 13 Flynns born into a family from the west coast.

Jerome and Daniel Flynn, with wet suits and snorkels, play games in the sea with Fungi the dolphin from Dingle Bay. The boatman threw a rope from the back of the boat and the two boys held on while he opened up the throttle. As they skimmed across and through the water Fungi appeared alongside his new-found friends.

On arriving at Dingle, the boys asked a local at the harbour how they could get out to Fungi. "Sure, there's only one man who can take you out this time of the year, and that will be Paddy Garvey. I know a man who knows where he lives". Jerome and Daniel found this man and asked him if he knew Paddy Garvey. "Very well", came the reply. "What will you be after?" "We want to swim with Fungi the dolphin and wondered if he could take us out to sea", Jerome said. "Well he normally likes to take a party of people in his boat at £5 a person", said the man. "Will you be able to make it worth his while?" "Certainly", replied Jerome, "how about £20. Will he accept that? Are you a friend of his?" "I am himself", replied the man delighted with the offer. "I am that Paddy Garvey."

Four times the boys made the trip out to sea, striking up a close friendship with both Fungi the dolphin and Paddy the boatman. By now Jerome was totally enthralled. It was another amazing experience. "Once Fungi had learned to trust us", he said, "he started to teach us how to play."

Inspired by a dolphin once again, Jerome returned to England and an interesting invitation from Central TV. Zelda Barron, a director, who had seen Jerome playing Orlando, had invited him to put on uniform and play the part of an officer in a drama series about the army. Jerome read the character references and immediately requested demotion — "probably", he said, "the first time a Sandhurst-trained soldier has ever preferred to be a squaddie. I didn't feel right with the part. Officers give orders and demand respect. I wanted to play a character that was more suited to the energy I felt I could give." He was then offered the part of an ordinary Lance Corporal, a big-hearted fellow who liked singing, climbing trees, drank a lot of beer and was always falling in love. That was nearer the mark and Jerome accepted.

A name was needed for the character and Zelda asked Jerome to make that decision himself. He thought for a while and his mind took him back to County Kerry and that boat trip to meet the dolphin. "Paddy Garvey", he said. "I would like to be Lance Corporal Paddy Garvey." Central loved the name and Jerome happily signed up for the seven-part series called *Soldier, Soldier,* wondering if the old Irish sea dog from Dingle Bay would ever know that his name was now, and for ever more, associated with the British Army!

Paddy Garvey, of Dingle Bay, in summer 1996.

In the first series of Soldier, Soldier, Lance Corporal Paddy Garvey quickly proved that he had the kind of warmth and humour that delighted the rank and file of the King's Fusiliers. Here is Jerome, on stage, in drag, entertaining the troops. Robson was not so impressed. "The most frightening moment in my life", he said, "was the day I saw Jerome in a bra!"

Rosie and Robson with his arm in a sling which had nothing to do with the Soldier, Soldier plot. He was shooting a scene when someone sat on his hand and dislocated his thumb. "It went crack", said Robson "and I ended up in casualty of all places. They wrenched it back but the bone was chipped. The next day I had to play a fight scene but those who looked closely will have seen that I only punched with my right hand."

4: Robson and Jerome Meet In A Taxi

AS the filming for *Soldier, Soldier* got under way, action-man Lance Corporal Paddy Garvey (Jerome Flynn) and the rebel comedian, Fusilier Dave Tucker (Robson Green) shared the same hotel but spoke to each other for the first time in the back of a taxi. Jerome remembers that first impression. "I was a bit nervous about meeting this guy", he said, "because I knew we would have to have a close relationship and I wasn't sure if we would really hit it off. Anyway, there he was in the taxi. I thought he looked a bit, sort of...weaselly!" Robson said: "I actually recognised him as he approached the taxi because I had seen him play Orlando at the Theatre Royal, Newcastle and he was brilliant. Then the taxi door opened, this great jaw and squashed nose sat down beside me and then the jaw opened and said, 'Hi'. I knew we had to have this instant rapport and be able to interact socially — and we did."

As the two actors read the script and then chatted they soon discovered they had one thing in common. They were pacifists. Not exactly the ideal qualification for a life of action in the King's Fusiliers. Now they had to handle guns, drive tanks, throw hand grenades and crawl on their bellies across mine fields. They kept reminding themselves that they were only actors and the ammunition was blanks — although they were both later to experience the harsh reality of army discipline.

The early rehearsals were supposed to be preceded by a week of intensive training but something went badly wrong. Jerome said: "All I did was jump over one wall on an assault course and then we all went to the pub with our military advisor which proved just as useful because that's where we began to bond. Jerome discovered that Robson was a great chatterbox. "I couldn't get a word in edgeways", he said, "but it didn't matter because Robson made me laugh and continues to make me laugh. He is one of the funniest guys I've ever met. He is like the dolphin. He celebrates life all the time and I can honestly say the room or bar is always more joyous if Robson is in it. He has everyone in stitches." On the other hand Robson found Jerome to be a calming influence but was a bit alarmed by the number of rehearsals he demanded. "He rehearsed to death", he said. "Today, it's the other way round."

This spirit of togetherness was infectious. Despite their vastly different backgrounds the talkative, clowning Robson and the jokey, peace-loving Jerome got to enjoy each other's company and that of other members of the cast. "In a way it was like the army", said Jerome. "Here we were, thrown together in adverse conditions, in winter, in Birmingham, everyone away from their family and friends, in a project we were all nervous about — playing soldiers!"

Although they were pacifists both Robson and Jerome appreciated the need for the army. "My grandad fought in two world wars", said Robson, "and educated me in such a way that I realised wars are fought by sinister powers and not by the actual people." Jerome agreed: "As a child I was told I was naïve when I said I couldn't understand why the army existed at all. Now I began to realise that it was a response to the needs of a very ill, self-obsessed society — as a peacekeeping force — but, within the army, there were some wonderful characters just as there are in any walk of life."

Ironically, a "sinister force" was already threatening to ruin this first series of *Soldier, Soldier.* As Robson and Jerome trained, rehearsed and met their fellow actors — all 68 of them — Saddam Hussein had declared war on Kuwait and hostilities in the Gulf commenced. Producer Chris Kelly and creator Lucy Gannon made the decision to postpone the screening on the ITV network, scheduled for January 1991, until the war was over.

Both actors were enjoying the work and the relationships they were striking up with the other actors around them, although they were still convinced the series would be a great big flop. "Robson and I became great friends", said Jerome "and the fun we had on camera made it all worthwhile." Jerome, as Paddy Garvey, was also relishing the physical work such as square-bashing, route marching and, of course, climbing trees and mountains. Robson, as Dave Tucker, was finding no difficulty in being the rebellious, scruffy character who was one of the lads but likely any moment to be kicked out of the army. Tucker had a screen wife, the tempestuous Donna, who loved wearing high heels, mini-skirts and going to discos and gave her husband a harder time than he received from the officers. She was played by Rosie Rowell, an expert Flamenco dancer who, like Jerome, graduated from Central.

Rosie was not originally in the series at all. The part of Donna had gone to Angie Clarke, an actress who dropped out at the last moment forcing Chris Kelly to ask those who had already been cast if they could recommend a good replacement. Robson and Rosie had mutual friends in Newcastle and he knew of her dancing ability, stage work and her first TV series *South of the Border.* He and Cathryn Harrison who played Laura Cadman both thought Rosie Rowell would make a perfect Donna and put her name forward. She was invited to an audition along with ten other girls and got the job.

Jerome's screen girlfriend at the start of the series was Corporal Nancy Thorpe, a military policewoman who had never charged or arrested anyone and had set her heart on the highly unsuitable Paddy Garvey. She was played by Holly Aird, an actress who began her TV career at the age of nine in the BBC series *The History of Mr Polly* and then went on to star alongside Hayley Mills in *The Flame Trees of Thika.* Holly's father was in the Royal Scots Guards and she was actually born in an army hospital at Aldershot.

Paddy Garvey and his girlfriend, Nancy Thorpe, the rather inadequate military police-woman played by Holly Aird. Jerome recalls how the more they got to know each other, the more difficult it was to keep a straight face and act responsibly. "In one scene with the two of us and Robson, the camera turned on Holly for the reverse camera shot, but we just couldn't keep it together and had to be sent out of the room. Holly acted the scene on her own with the director reading our lines.
We were waiting outside, in disgrace."

The first series of *Soldier, Soldier,* screened in the autumn of 1991, was a colossal success attracting an audience in excess of nine million viewers a week and reaching number seven in the ITV ratings. At the Houston International Film Festival it won the gold award for the best drama series and, among those 68 actors, the principal characters to emerge were Garvey, Tucker, Nancy and Donna along with Sergeant Tony Wilton (Gary Love) and Major Tom Cadman (David Haig).

Jerome wasn't too pleased at having to appear naked on the parade ground in one scene but he enjoyed his first screen kiss from Holly Aird. He said: "Robson, Gary and I became great mates and Holly was a riot to work with. Kissing Holly was no problem at all, great fun, and I got paid for it." He also enjoyed the occasion when, as Garvey, he climbed a tree, considerably the worse for drink and, from the top, serenaded Nancy with the song *Danny Boy*. Robson loved the emotional, tragic and vulnerable side of Dave Tucker who was court-martialled in the sixth episode for striking a superior officer. He also enjoyed portraying Tucker's extraordinary relationship with the flamboyant, disco-loving Donna.

The resounding success of *Soldier, Soldier* meant another series and a shedding of the cast which the directors admitted had been far too large. Some prominent actors left voluntarily, but that did not bother the creator Lucy Gannon or Chris Kelly because they realised that army personnel come and go all the time. The first series was filmed in Staffordshire. Now the King's Fusiliers would be moving to Hong Kong. Robson was pleased and Jerome delighted. It was an opportunity to work with Robson again and travel and explore. His father's family had lived in Hong Kong after the war, having been interned in a POW camp in Shanghai from 1943-1945.

In early 1990 Jerome arranged a surprise treat for his mother for her 50th birthday. She flew to Newcastle and was fitted out with a wet suit. The next day Jerome told her she would be swimming in the sea with Freddie the Dolphin. Fern will never forget that February day. "It was bitterly cold", she said, "but we took a small boat to the end of the harbour at Amble and there was Freddie, cavorting and leaping. I lowered myself in the freezing water and enjoyed this wonderful experience. I even touched him for a moment. It was typical of Jerome to have thought of something like that for a present."

Three great series with Casualty and the time comes to leave. Here is Robson with some of the cast of the popular TV drama series. Before he said goodbye there was one very awkward moment for Robson and that was when Jerome made a guest appearance in Casualty. "I was talking to the hospital receptionist on camera", said Jerome, "when the door opened and Robson came past with his porter's trolley. I nearly corpsed, it was so weird not seeing him in army uniform. Mercifully, we didn't have to speak to each other. That would have been impossible."

Anne Green's "wonderful surprise" came in the summer of 1992 when Robson announced that he had bought her an airline ticket and she would join him in Hong Kong. Anne toured the city, saw all the sights, enjoyed many Chinese meals and watched some of the shooting of Soldier, Soldier. "It was", she said, "the trip of a lifetime."

WITH the first series of *Soldier, Soldier* completed, Robson continued with *Casualty* and also returned to the stage. In one of the plays, *And a Nightingale Sang* with the Northern Stage Company, he portrayed a World War II soldier and, in another, he took the part of Jesus in the *York Mystery Plays*. By this time Robson was told that Central TV were making another series of *Soldier, Soldier*. "Where will you be filming", he inquired, a little unsure whether he wanted to continue. "Hong Kong", came the answer. "I'm packing my bags", said Robson, knowing now that he could no longer continue with *Casualty*. In some ways it was obviously right to leave, for Jimmy the porter had not been invited to train as a nurse or doctor, as Robson had hoped he might, and he felt he had gone as far as he could with the character. But he still found the decision difficult. "I had been with the team for three great series", he said. "Many people told me I was making a big mistake in quitting such a highly successful prime time show and the economic stability it provided. It was a more difficult decision than leaving the shipyard."

Robson completed his last episode of *Casualty* on a Thursday and the next day flew to Hong Kong where Jerome was already planning to find the grave of the paternal grandfather he had never met. A break in filming gave him the opportunity to look at his father's old school and visit the city cemetery. "There were about 30,000 graves", he said. "It was an impossible task but I am sure that George knew I had made the effort to find him."

Robson also had his difficulties. In one scene he refused to jump into a boat as it was pulling away, insisting that stunt men were employed for those sort of things but he did agree to leap out of a tree into a lagoon 20 feet below wearing Y-fronts, a pair of boots and nothing else.

More alarmingly, Robson and Jerome, the whole cast of *Soldier Soldier* and the production team were terrified of the Hong Kong mafia — the notorious Triads who demanded money in return for location shots in city streets and alleys. Robson said: "Chris Kelly was asked to cough up thousands of pounds to film in a certain road and, to prevent him doing so, a Triad stood in front of the camera until he either paid or went away. The police apparently were powerless. It was extortion of the worst kind."

The second series was shown on their return to England and it was again so successful that the network asked the producers for a third run and said this time they would like 13 episodes. Robson and Jerome signed on again and so did most of the main cast, amid rumours that they might be going to New Zealand.

A rare serious moment for Robson at 33,000 feet and Jerome in Hong Kong with Annabelle Apsion, who plays Joy Wilton. They all thought that Soldier Soldier might be a flop but it was a huge success and that only helped to improve the tremendous camaraderie that already existed between the actors and the crew. Jerome said: "Robson and I began to sing together on set, between the scenes, mainly to keep our energy and enthusiasm up. It was then we discovered that we had the same taste in music."

Robson and Jerome in Hong Kong, wading through a river on the left and above, obviously enjoying themselves in full camouflage gear. They often had to remind each other that they weren't in a Dad's Army episode and this was the serious side of army life. But it was difficult. The temptation was to ham it up, to overplay and they increasingly found it difficult to take each other seriously as actors. Such was the infectiousness of the fun that Robson and Jerome instilled on camera that, on one occasion, in a very butch soldier scene, even the director cracked up.

TRUE to form Jerome fell in love with New Zealand and immediately felt at home. It was a continuation of the spiritual journey which had been prompted by the dolphin meeting and, in New Zealand, he sensed an energy which made him feel very much in tune with the planet as a whole. "Despite everything they have suffered through loss of rights and integration, some Maoris have still managed to hold on to their indigenous beliefs and values", he said. "We were lucky enough to have several Maoris in the film crew, travelling with us. They were naturally very spiritual people, more in tune with themselves and their environment than anyone I've met. The practice of healing through touch is traditionally passed down the female line."

Robson also loved New Zealand and remembers how he was taken to the location deep in the outback and, on the first evening, went with some friends to the village bar patronised by several farmers. "I saw them look at me in a strange way and then glance at the television in the corner of the room", he said. "There were more double takes and then I noticed they were watching me in *Casualty*."

Soon after they arrived and settled down at an army camp at Waiouru in the middle of the North Island, they were invited by the Maoris to their land for a welcoming ceremony. The *Soldier, Soldier* team rubbed noses with the whole of the local tribe who then sang and told stories. A Maori in the crew replied on behalf of the actors. It was a novel and moving experience for all of them and, although they didn't understand the language, the singing was beautiful. As they were about to leave a very large Maori mamma took Jerome in her arms and gave him one of the biggest hugs he had ever known. "I felt this energy and love surging through my body", he said. "It was a kind of healing experience. All I could do was cry."

On another occasion Robson, Jerome, Gary Love and two others were taken white water rafting and told they were going to a grade five river. "Is that good or bad?", asked Robson. "It's exciting", replied the Kiwi guide. It was actually too exciting. As they bounced round a bend in the river they noticed to their horror that the rapids disappeared ahead of them into a watery chasm. "We hit the waterfall", said Robson, "the boat flipped and I went out and under and I couldn't get up. I was trapped in an air pocket and all around me were bubbles. I started screaming and Gary somehow managed to pull me out. The coach journey back home took three hours and no-one said a word — we were all so shattered." The next day the five actors reported for duty determined not to say too much about their frightening escapade but immediately received a memo from the director: "No more white water rafting."

Rather disappointingly, only three episodes of *Soldier, Soldier* were made in New Zealand. For the remaining ten, the Kings Fusiliers moved to Münster in Germany and, for the first time, were based in real army barracks belonging to the 1st Battalion of the Coldstream Guards. For Jerome this provided another experience he will remember.

Golf under the volcano at Waiouru, North Island, New Zealand. The game was played amid wisecracks, laughter and lots of singing — but neither of them remembers who actually won. Robson and Jerome and, in fact, all the Soldier, Soldier cast felt as if they had been through a great spiritual experience after New Zealand. It brought them even closer together.

The success of Soldier, Soldier was earning for Robson and Jerome thousands of female admirers, invitations to appear on TV chat shows and scores of requests for interviews from all sections of the media. The eco-friendly Jerome, with his spiritual quests in Hong Kong and New Zealand and his affinity with whales and dolphins was particularly in demand and he became adept at providing the right quote for the right occasion. In one full interview Jerome admitted that he "was still trying to find himself" — a comment that caused great amusement among his friends. During a cricket match at Ide Hill a few days after the newspaper article was published, a fielder called out from deep square leg — "any clues yet Jerome?"

Dave Tucker gets it in the ear from Company Sergeant Major Michael Stubbs, played by Rob Spendlove. Tucker was frequently in trouble and so was Robson. In Hong Kong he noticed that Miles Anderson, who played Lt Col Dan Fortune, actually got saluted by the real soldiers, so Robson borrowed Miles' hat and walked towards the parade ground to see if he could have the same effect on the men. To his horror an RMP saw him "impersonating an officer" and had him frogmarched to the cells with Robson protesting that he was "only an actor and his director should be told immediately what was happening". Robson was locked away, still complaining, unaware that the whole "unfortunate episode" was set-up by his mates with Jerome as ringleader!

Three photographs borrowed from Robson's scrapbook show him with Mo Sesay who played Fusilier 'Midnight' Rawlings, Jerome "in search of the sky" and Rob with his mum Anne in Hong Kong.

THE real-life Münster-based soldiers of the Coldstream Guards gave a cautious welcome to the team of actors masquerading as the King's Fusiliers, sharing their barracks, trucks, tanks — but not rifles. In this part of the third series the story-line showed the Fusiliers merging with the Cumbrians to form a rapid reaction force for the United Nations and naturally Paddy Garvey and Dave Tucker were in the thick of action. In one incident Paddy was thrown into the cells and, in order to play the part with accuracy, Jerome volunteered for similar treatment. "I thought it would help me to understand this aspect of military life", he said.

It was, however, a terrifying experience. "Real military policemen had me marching, running on the spot, scrubbing floors, doing press ups", said Jerome. "It was hell. Then they forced me to run around the exercise yard carrying this huge cannon shell. It was a relief when they finally threw me in the cell."

What was slightly alarming for Jerome was that the Coldstream Guards weren't acting. He was no different in their eyes from the other squaddies they arrested. He could at any time have told them to stop but he accepted the punishment so as not to lose respect.

They were in Germany for four months and attracted huge crowds of supporters wherever they went. Jerome said: "The situation was actually rather delicate because the Coldstream Guards were preparing to go to Bosnia and, at the same time, sharing their barracks with a load of actors prancing around and pretending to know what military life was all about."

Between the transmission of the third series (from September 1993) and the filming of the fourth, Jerome appeared in a prime-time episode of the TV drama *Between The Lines* in which he played the lover of Lesley Vicarage, who was also 2nd Lieutenant Kate Butler in *Soldier, Soldier*. Lesley, particularly, was looking forward to the fourth series, filmed in Cyprus, because her character was to be significantly in the spotlight. Kate's affair with Captain Kieran Voce, the working class lad who had risen through the ranks, played by Dorian Healy, meant that wedding bells were in the air.

In Cyprus the cast had a hotel to themselves next to the sea and Robson and Jerome took full advantage, swimming, sunbathing and exploring on every possible occasion. One day they found a rock jutting out into the Mediterranean, miles from anywhere and spent several hours on it, between swims, singing old Elvis and Beatles numbers. To amuse themselves they decided that, if desperate, they could make an album called *Ling along with Rob and Rome.* "We found it a wonderfully funny idea", said Jerome. "and as time went on our 'album' became a running joke."

They returned to England and the time came to film the *Soldier Soldier* wedding. The story-line made it clear that Kate and Kieran were so popular that the squaddies had clubbed together and booked a band for the wedding reception but no-one ever imagined that the sequence which followed would take its place in television folklore. The band never turned up but Garvey and Tucker did, arguing on stage about who was "to play Cliff". They sang *Unchained Melody.* The emotional impact was heightened by the fact that Donna was having an affair with her art teacher and Dave was likely to lose her.

Robson remembers the production meeting which preceded filming: "It was our idea to sing because Jerome and I were always singing off set and annoying the crew. We put the idea to the directors and they agreed. We wanted to do a quick rhythm and blues number but it was Annie Tricklebank, the producer's idea that we should sing *Unchained Melody.* Robson said: *"Unchained Melody* is like its title. It's delicate. The melody moves about. We were very frightened."

The episode in this fourth series appeared on British television in October 1994. The next day record shops all over England informed their respective head offices that *Soldier, Soldier* fans were trying to buy a copy of *Unchained Melody* sung by Robson Green and Jerome Flynn. The news reached the giant Recording Company of America (RCA) and Simon Cowell, of the Artistes and Repertoire Department, was put in charge of tracking down the boys.

By now *Soldier, Soldier* viewing figures were more than 16 million and Jerome and Robson had a following that included thousands of real squaddies all over England. The majority of fans, however, were female and many wrote to their heroes saying how much they loved the series and the song and urged them not to leave. But Jerome particularly was getting restless and warned the producers of his desire to quit. "I never intended to continue in *Soldier Soldier* for so long. I don't think any of us did. But before we knew it we had been to six different countries and five years had just flown past That showed how much fun we were having."

Despite the jollity and the exotic locations the boys were keen to put their energies behind some fresh projects either together, or alone. It didn't matter. In fact, offers of work were pouring in and both had passions to pursue. Robson was keen to encourage re-investment in the arts in the north-east whether it be theatre, television or film through his company, Coastal Productions. Jerome had his head full of ideas concerning the environment. He was disturbed about the whales being slaughtered using the excuse that it was in the interest of scientific research. He actually wanted to join the Greenpeace crew on their mission in Japanese waters, until he realised he would only be of any use as a cook.

Central, however, dangled a carrot in front of the boys by telling them the next series would start in Australia and finish in South Africa. It was too exciting to turn down. Jerome said he would do the first part of the series. Robson said he would leave at the end. With their immediate professional future sealed Robson went home to Newcastle and Jerome made arrangements to spend a quiet Christmas with his new girlfriend Anna, prior to leaving in January for a retreat in India and Nepal.

Robson junior and senior after Newcastle's drubbing of Antwerp in an early round of the UEFA Cup in the 1994-5 season. They won 5-0.

DENISE in the sales department of RCA continued to keep Simon Cowell well informed of the frustrations being suffered by retailers all over the country. "*Unchained Melody* by Robson and Jerome? Very sorry but the record has never been released. We'll let you know if the boys change their minds." Cowell was now determined not to let the opportunity escape but he was having a difficult time. He contacted Annie Tricklebank, series producer of *Soldier, Soldier* and learned, to his delight, that the boys shared the same theatrical agent, Kate Feast. He thought it would make his job a lot easier; in fact the opposite was the case because Kate quickly assured him that neither Robson nor Jerome was interested in making a record. Simon continued to ring Kate's London office, telling her that the song could make a Christmas number one, but the message was clear — "you haven't a cat in hell's chance of getting them to change their minds."

Simon's usually sunny profile deserted him and he went on holiday depressed but determined to persevere after Christmas. He tried a new tack — Anne Green, Robson's mum. "Please talk to your son and tell him to contact me. He could soon be on Top of the Pops." After 300 telephone calls to the director, the agent, Mrs Green and other close friends of the boys Simon's persistence finally paid off. Robson rang the RCA office in Fulham and told the record producer firmly that he was an actor, not a singer, and would rather not be put in a position where he would have to appear on Top of the Pops. Simon explained the advance he was prepared to offer and Robson's voice went weak. "That's a lot of money."

Robson and Simon spoke on the telephone again in Kate Feast's office when Robson explained that he would make the record only if Jerome agreed. But Jerome was on a pilgrimage in the mountains under the mystical spell of meditation, totally at home and at peace in his retreat — a world away from soldiers, record producers and pop stars. His only contact with the late twentieth century was a fax machine in the village. Robson, though, had his number. "Jerome 'phone me urgently. Need to speak to you."

Jerome found a telephone and rang Robson. The boys have a perfect memory of the conversation that followed:
"Rob, it's Rome. What do you want?"
"Hello, Jerome. How's your mind?"
"Peaceful, thanks Rob."
"Oh, that's nice. How's your voice?"
"Not so good."
"Well, start gargling. Go and buy some Strepsils."
"They don't sell 'em around here. Why?"
"Because we're on Top of the Pops in a month's time."

"Rob, I thought you weren't interested, and now I've had time to think about it, I'm not interested either."

"But, Jerome. There's a lot of money involved."

"How much?"

"£50,000."

"Rob. I'm going to find a chemist!"

The boys had at least now agreed to talk. Jerome flew home from India to the RCA offices where he met Robson. "As we went up in the lift to Simon Cowell's office", said Robson, "we were convinced we were going to meet a typical cynical record producer with spikey blond hair and dark glasses. In fact he was a good laugh and sincere and, amazingly, we shared the same taste in music." Simon also remembers that meeting. "Robson was leaping around all over the place, coming out with funny lines and twitching with excitement. Jerome was spaced out by a mixture of jet lag, the effects of meditation, tiredness and confusion. I suggested they record *Unchained Melody* and follow it up with an album later in the year over which they would have complete artistic control on the choice of the songs. They agreed to sign up."

RCA's A and R Man, Simon Cowell (left) with Robson, Jerome and Hugh Goldsmith (MD) on the day they signed the deal. In Simon's office the boys are known as Prozak and Twiddler because Robson is always "leaping around like someone who is on Prozak" and Jerome "twiddles and tweaks to try to improve the records."

WITH the deal completed, recording arrangements established and the basic structure of a video to accompany the single agreed in principle, Robson and Jerome flew to Australia to begin filming their fifth and final series of *Soldier, Soldier.* They very nearly didn't come back. A riptide, a cyclone, a burning aircraft and a desert storm — all real life dramas — contrived to imperil the lives of the two young men. They were moments that still make their flesh tingle when they think about them.

Jerome recalled the first incident: "We were in a coastal town called Catherine Hill Bay and, after we finished filming, Robson, Anna and I rushed down our lunch and ran down to the sea. The surf was great and I'm a surfing addict but we got caught in this riptide. Robson managed to struggle out but Anna and I were in trouble. We had stomachs full of food and had to swim against the current. The waves turned us over several times and we had absolutely no energy left when a huge wave finally threw us up on the sand."

The adventures Down Under continued. The story-line showed the King's Own Fusiliers caught in a dramatic storm so the directors hired hundreds of extras and the crew bought tons of tackle, rain and wind machines in an attempt to simulate a cyclone — then a real cyclone blew up, a violent affair which made everyone aware of the power of nature, Aussie style. It was far too dangerous to film so they had to return the next day and set up all the equipment again.

A few days later filming switched to the middle of the Australian outback near Alice Springs and Robson and Jerome took a day off to fly to the famous Ayres Rock for some publicity photographs. In the tiny single-engined aircraft were the two boys, the photographer and a green young pilot called Jamie who was trying to build up his flying hours and could only navigate by following mountains, water-holes and other natural landmarks.

When they left the plane, the pilot told them to be back at six o'clock because he didn't have enough experience to fly in the dark and sunset was at seven. So the three set off to climb the massive mound of red rock that rose several hundred feet out of the desert unaware that the photographer's watch was an hour slow because he had forgotten to adjust it after arriving at Alice Springs. This meant that they arrived back at the airstrip way after the scheduled time to find Jamie in a panic because it was almost dark and he could see a storm coming.

Jerome said: "We had been in the air for two minutes when Jamie turned to us with fear in his eyes. Sweat was pouring from his face and he said 'Hey, can you guys smell burning?' We sniffed and screamed at him. 'Yes'." As the boys put their arms over their heads and waited for the aircraft to explode Jamie

"Release what?
Unchained Melody as a single?
"We're actors, not pop stars. What
a funny idea! But thanks for
ringing. It's a great laugh."

When the boys first heard of RCA's suggestion that they should make a single of Unchained Melody it was Jerome who said that they should at least listen to what Simon Cowell was prepared to offer. But Robson disagreed. He was frightened about the idea of two actors making a pop record and what it might do for their credibility. "I gave up trying to persuade him", said Jerome, "went to India and was rather surprised to receive a fax urging me to phone him immediately."

banked the plane, made an emergency landing and discovered the smell had been caused by the rubber wheels spinning on the tarmac. "It was the first time since I've known Robson", said Jerome, "that he wasn't able to make me laugh." Robson agreed: "A plane crash was enough but the crashing and burning at the same time was too much."

Their adventure was not over. As Jamie took off again it was dark. He had no proper navigational equipment or lights to guide him across the desert and the storm was getting closer. The plane began to wobble as the wind picked up and the boys could see lightning hitting the red earth which was glistening in the rain. Jerome also saw a complete circular rainbow — a sensational sight which Robson missed because he was too busy changing his underpants! Jamie had tried to fly round the edge of the storm but in doing so he had become completely lost. The desert darkness offered him no help at all. After an hour they eventually saw the lights of the Alice Springs runway. As they came into land Jerome said to Robson that it was a bit like being in a video game. It was Jamie who replied: "Naah mate, it's a lot harder."

Another problem with Australia was the flies. "They were awful", said Robson. I would be chatting away doing a scene and I'd have to stop everyone and say "Sorry, can we cut, I've got a bluebottle stuck in my larynx."

Jerome particularly enjoyed this final series because Anna was with him and also it meant working again with Holly Aird, who played his former wife Nancy. In fact it was Jerome who persuaded the producers to bring her back and he collaborated with them over the story-line. "Paddy Garvey had never got over losing Nance", he said, "and after two years of painful separation he desperately wanted her back. Fortunately the producers thought it was a good idea." So did Holly.

The final chapter in *Soldier, Soldier* as far as Jerome and Holly were concerned was the second wedding of Paddy and Nancy, the culmination of one of television drama's most cliff-hanging love affairs. It ended with both of them crying, real tears. Holly had got caught up with the emotion and Jerome was sad that he was leaving *Soldier, Soldier* and, particularly the crew and his mates. But he knew it was the right thing to do. As far as the producers were concerned, however, his posting overseas left the way open for Corporal Paddy Garvey to march back one day into the ranks of the King's Own Fusiliers.

The culmination of a long on-screen love affair.

*In February and early March 1995, Robson Green appeared on TV
screens as Rory Connor in a three-part adaptation of Catherine
Cookson's The Gambling Man. The author, whose books, about
everyday life during her youth, are romantic rather than sentimen-
tal, comes from Robson's own part of England — so the Geordie
connection continued. There was a memorable "fire sequence" in the
film and Robson, who played the leading character, naturally had a
stunt double to do the dangerous stuff. "It was great fun", he said,
"one of my favourite moments in my career so far. We had the special effects people from London's Burning to deal with the fire."*

While Robson was making The Gambling Man, Jerome was appearing in an Anglia Television production of the P D James TV drama, A Mind to Murder, in which he played the villain. The play had a dramatic ending showing Jerome being chased across sand dunes and marshes and then sinking in a sea of mud. Unlike Robson, Jerome loves the adventurous stuff and certainly did not want a stunt man to take his place. The photograph shows the dramatic scene, with Roy Marsden, the star of the series, attempting to save the villain in order that he could face his punishment.

*Robson went to South Africa without Jerome but, in Nasha's Farm,
found a friend who, he said, had a similar bone structure!*

5: The Unlikely Lads

*O*h, *my love, my darling, I hunger for your touch...* The unmistakable voices of the Righteous Brothers singing the incomparable words of *Unchained Melody* drifted out of Simon Cowell's car stereo. The A and R man, on holiday at the time, was listening to the treatment of the song by the group who took it to number one thirty years earlier. He let the tape run and after a few more songs the lyrics of another emotive number came over loud and clear — *"There'll be Bluebirds over the White Cliffs of Dover, Tomorrow just you wait and see..."* Simon stopped the car and the thoughts tumbled around his head. "That's it. That's the other side. It's the 50th anniversary of Victory in Europe on May 8th. We'll release the single as a double A on that date. We can't go wrong."

The year of Robson and Jerome was already underway but, thanks to the charismatic Cowell, his energy and ideas, the most incredible phase had yet to start. The boys flew back from Australia and within days had been introduced to the legendary musicians Mike Stock and Matt Aitken and their studio. "They were my first choice to produce the record", said Simon. "They have golden ears for a pop opportunity and understand the market." Stock and Aitken who have a £4 million studio complex in London's Southwark spent the seventies and early eighties as session musicians, honing their guitar keyboard. In 1984 they went into production. Before they met Robson and Jerome their arrangement skills had given them 13 number one singles — the last one being Kylie Minogue's *Tears On My Pillow*. They were now confident of the fourteenth.

Stock and Aitken and Robson and Jerome sound like a couple of comedy double acts and, in a way, they are but between the quips and the jokes, the agonies and the frustrations, the recordings were completed. "We didn't know how it was going", said Robson, "until we heard the first playback from White Cliffs of Dover. Jerome was also convinced. "Mate", he said, "our lives are never going to be the same again!"

The release date was fixed for Monday May 8th, 1995 (VE Day plus 50 years) but the doubts lingered on. Despite Simon Cowell's unwavering conviction that the record would make the charts both Robson and Jerome knew that *Unchained Melody* had been used in the film *Ghost* not so long ago and the Righteous Brothers had been in the charts with their 1965 recording. It had also been a hit for Jimmy Young and the American pianist Liberace. The boys decided that they really had nothing to lose. They were actors, not pop singers.

For the video to accompany the record they were told they could choose their own director and come up with their own idea for a script. The first was easy. As director of *The Gambling Man*, Norman Stone, a former BBC man had cast Robson as Rory and the two had enjoyed a splendid working relationship. Norman had also directed such artists as Pink Floyd, Cliff Richard and Duran Duran and that experience was invaluable. So the tables were turned and Norman Stone was chosen as director of the first (and subsequent) Robson and Jerome videos. "I had two chaps who could act as well as sing", he said, "and unlike most pop stars they were not afraid of the camera. This gave me an opportunity to tell a story with a beginning, middle and end through the four-minute video."

The idea for a good script was a little more difficult but eventually it was decided to link *Unchained Melody* with the war-time film *Brief Encounter*, starring Trevor Howard and Celia Johnson while *White Cliffs* would depict the return of peace at the end of the second world war, Terry Waite's first taste of freedom, the fall of the Berlin wall and Nelson Mandela's release from prison. They were brilliant and RCA loved them. "The only problem I had", Norman said, "was getting the boys to be serious. They only really calmed down when they were tired."

Things began to happen fast. Jerome's sister Kerry, aware of her brother's difficulty in trying to reply individually to hundreds of letters from all over the country decided to start a Robson and Jerome fan club from her home in Northumberland. She sent details of the club to all who had written, requesting name, address and age and was delighted when the first member signed up a few days later — Marjorie Atkinson, aged 79. Within a few weeks more than a thousand had joined and Kerry rented an office, bought computers and took on staff to deal with orders for signed photographs, posters and T-shirts, and to despatch the club's official newsletter *Fanfare*. By Christmas, 1995 the membership had leapt to an incredible 6,000.

RCA did not want too many music-based radio and TV shows to play the record before the official launch date but there was one request which was too good to miss. The mother of one of the boys' fans — Melissa Svensen — had written to Cilla Black's show *Surprise, Surprise* asking if it would be possible for her daughter to meet her idol, Jerome. The producers of London Weekend Television approached RCA reminding them that it was an opportunity for *Unchained Melody* to have a first public airing a week before the record was due to be released.

As Robson and Jerome were waiting in the wings for Cilla Black to introduce them to Melissa and her sister, the occasion proved all too overwhelming for the boys. "I was frightened", said Jerome, "but Robson was petrified. We were used to acting but now we had to sing in front of a television audience of 14 million and Rob didn't want to go on. He was actually bent over double with nerves. I tried to get spiritual with him, reminding him how large the world was and how

Melissa (left) and Julia with the lads after the Surprise Surprise show. Below Robson and Jerome with Cilla and Jerome's mum, Fern.

Unchained Melody was written by Alex North and Hy Zaret for a little-known American film called *Unchained* in 1955. It was then chosen by Jimmy Young for a UK release in the same year. Today it is owned by Paul McCartney's publishing company MPL which acquired it in the early 1980s as part of the Frank Music Corporation Catalogue.

small and insignificant we were. That's the only way I could put everything into perspective."

Jerome's advice must have worked. Some months later, after the song had been released, the boys were booked to appear on the *Des O'Connor Show* and Robson, in another state of pre-show panic, said to Jerome "Tell me about the perspective again please, quickly!"

As May 8th approached Simon Cowell's instincts told him that the advance orders from the record shops of 150,000 — unheard of for a debut single — still might not be enough. He was right. The record went into the shops and out again. There were stampedes from Carlisle to Cornwall, from Lowestoft to Llandudno and, by the end of the first day, repeat orders exceeded an unprecedented 300,000. In Sevenoaks, Jerome's home town, there was a small scuffle on the shop floor of Woolworths as desperate female fans fought over the last available copy, a situation not quite in keeping with the spirit of peace and sisterly love appropriate to VE Day.

By the end of that week *Unchained Melody* had achieved one of the fastest first-week sales in the history of pop music — and it was on course to go straight in at number one. Incredibly, all this happened without any help from BBC Radio One, the pop music station, which refused to play the record because in their view it wasn't good or trendy enough and that Robson, 31, and Jerome, 32, were too old to be pop stars. But they had to play it on the evening of Sunday May 14th and every Sunday after that for seven weeks.

The Chart Show, dominated at the time by popular bands such as Pulp, Oasis and Take That, was presented as usual by Mark Goodier on that sunny Sunday evening in May. Unknown to him there were thousands of people listening to the programme who hadn't tuned in to the Chart Show since their teens. Among them was a fair representation of the 17 million *Soldier, Soldier* viewers and fan club members all over the country, desperate to hear if the song would make the top ten. Jerome was playing cricket at Ide Hill. Robson was in Bray, near Windsor in his rented Thameside house.

Jerome, in fact, had a problem. He was playing against his greatest rivals, Buckhurst CC, and soon after the programme began he was required to bat to help save the game for his side. His family and a dozen close friends were on the pavilion balcony, ears glued to the transistor radio and only occasionally glancing up at the game. Jerome wanted to be with them, but his sporting instincts told him it was a good day to score one of his famous fifties. Fate, however, took a hand. The hero of the hour was clean bowled by a former Wildernesse School mate for one. One was a good omen and he returned to the pavilion in time to hear Goodier move towards the famous countdown.

Some miles away to the west, Robson and Alison were in the garden of their house at Windsor as the Radio One presenter announced the top ten in reverse order.... "No 5, Oasis; No 4, Scatman; No 3, Guaglione; No 2 Dreamer...and straight in at number one with their debut single of *Unchained Melody* are *Soldier, Soldier* actors Robson Green and Jerome Flynn... *"Oh my love, my darling, I hunger..."*

Jerome's half brother and sister, Johnny and Lillie were at the cricket match on Sunday May 14th.

It was possibly the first time in cricket history that a pop song had halted play. There were hugs and handshakes for Jerome from players of both sides as a dozen champagne corks popped in unison. A three-second vision for ever frozen in Jerome's mind was the sight of a group of his mates. One was crying, another was laughing, almost uncontrollably, and the rest were cheering. To a man they were the same friends who had booed him off stage when he began to sing at the Ide Hill cricket club dance more than 10 years earlier. "That moment alone", said Jerome, "made it all worthwhile for me."

For Robson and Alison celebrations were a little quieter but there followed a moment to treasure. The elderly man next door popped his head over the garden fence, smiled and handed Robson a card. On one side was a picture of carrots, all smiling. On the other, a small message which read: "Congratulations. You are making a lot of old people very happy. It's about time that someone sang a song with a tune — Fred."

The euphoria didn't stop there. By the end of the second week the million sales landmark was already in sight and Robson and Jerome had the fastest selling record since Band Aid a decade previously. The pop world was stunned; the music industry had been turned upside down by two guys who had never wanted to be pop stars."

By now Robson and Jerome had sold 1.84 million copies and the record was the fastest selling single of the nineties. They also discovered that their singing had given one devoted fan, Heather Potts, her first spell of consciousness since a car crash the previous week that had left her in a coma. They donated five per cent of their royalties to Greenpeace which meant the handing over of a cheque for £18,000. And that gave Jerome particular pleasure. "The environment we live in is everything we have", he said. "In fact we're not separate from it. Greenpeace is desperate to preserve the environment from the constant abuse we throw at it. Therefore helping Greenpeace is helping ourselves".

A few weeks after Unchained Melody had lost its place on Top of The Pops, Robson and Jerome met Greenpeace activists outside the French embassy in Knightsbridge to make their personal protest against French nuclear testing in the Pacific and to hand over a cheque for £18,000 as part of the royalties from the single. Greenpeace, funded purely by individual donations was delighted to learn that another cheque would be forthcoming in December (in fact it was for £9,000 making a total of £27,000).

Double Emmy award-winning film director Norman Stone, who directed all the boys' videos, shows Robson the right eye line during filming of the Unchained Melody video at the Blue Bell railway station.

Anne Green was at home in Burradon with her daughters when it was announced that Robson and Jerome's Unchained Melody was Number One in the charts. Below: Robson senior and Uncle Billy (wheelchair bound because of an earlier mining accident and Robson junior's number one supporter) are seen in the garden with their racing pigeons.

Jerome, clean bowled for one, walks towards the pavilion in time to hear the Radio One countdown. Left: Outside the pavilion and on the mobile to Robson.

The crew of Soldier, Soldier always believed that Unchained Melody would be a massive hit if the boys released it — so they deserved the champagne, or what was left of it!

Remarkably, the massive sales success of *Unchained Melody* and *White Cliffs* was achieved with virtually no support from radio. According to Media Monitor the single was played only 37 times in its first week from 56 stations monitored. This meant it was exposed to a total audience of only 949,000 people — a seventieth of the exposure given to the week's top spins and nowhere near enough to earn it a place among the top 200. Fox FM played the record 15 times which left 22 among the other 55 stations. It was a phenomenon that completely baffled the music world.

In the second week, with VE celebrations still taking place, radio responded to the runaway success with 216 plays for *Unchained Melody* and NONE at all for *White*

Cliffs of Dover. Mike Stock and Matt Aitken who produced the record also had a number eight hit in America at the same time which made it their best week ever in an illustrious career. And for Simon Cowell, *Unchained Melody* was his first number one — a great reward for his determination in getting the boys to sign a contract. It also meant that eight different versions of the song had been a hit, something no other song could match.

RCA sales manager Steve Reeves who reported first week's sales figures of 310,000 told the music press that the market had gone berserk. This was followed by 460,000 copies in the second week and 320,000 in the third which meant the single had already become a million seller and Robson and Jerome had won three platinum awards.

6: *The Boys Make Pop History*

THE year of Robson and Jerome was moving on fast. The boys had been news for many months but now they were features. Double-page spreads in the nationals and colour supplements were augmented by long television interviews with reporters and presenters desperate to explore every perspective and find a few more. Much was made of a comment that they "loved each other", leaving Robson to explain that they were both heterosexuals but really great friends. "Men can say I love you but they don't. There's a macho stigma to men expressing their feelings which I've never understood. If you tell people you love them it makes them feel special. It's more important than any amount of money". Jerome agreed: "We have a very special relationship and the only thing I dislike about Robson is the way he sometimes takes the ball off me when we play football."

Sex Symbols, Greenpeace Warriors, Chartbusters, Luvvy-Duvvies, The Army Cor! The headlines rolled on and on and so did the TV appearances including Top of the Pops — the Thursday evening live chart show which they had to attend frequently because they were number one for seven weeks. Despite Robson's earlier reservations about TOTP he loved it, although he felt sick in his dressing room from nerves before every appearance. They were mobbed frequently by screaming fans outside Television Centre. "It was weird because we were blokes in our thirties and we had 15-year-old girls screaming at us", said Robson. Jerome agreed: "It was a mixture of emotions. One moment we were terrified and the next on the edge of hysterical laughter."

The boys were no longer playing hard to get as far as Simon Cowell and RCA were concerned and readily agreed to launch another single and an album for Christmas together with a video to be directed by Norman Stone. But what should they sing on the A side of the single? Was there any tune ever written that could possibly be a serious follow-up to *Unchained Melody*? Robson, his mind racing back a few decades, was in no doubt as to his choice. It had to be *I Believe* — the ballad that put The Bachelors on the musical map in the sixties and that was sung by Frankie Laine, Tom Jones, Dolly Parton and, most passionately of all, by Robson Green senior in the Dudley Working Mens' Club all those years ago. *I Believe* — the hit which was outselling The Beatles in 1964 before Robson junior could walk!

Simon began to make the essential copyright inquiries and with help from the *Daily Mirror* discovered that it had been written for a movie actress by four struggling American scriptwriters who were working on a sit-com called *USA Canteen* and were told to put together a catchy number for the leading lady's Thanksgiving scene. One of them was Ervin Drake who went on to write 30 other hits. The song was a success on the show and CBS wanted the actress Jane Froman to release it as a single. She said at the time: "It's very nice material for a television show but it's got no commercial value." Instead, 50s recording artist Frankie Laine released it and sold 12 million copies. The Bachelors then sold another million with their version and over the years the total has moved on to 25 million — one of the most phenomenal single sales of all time. The ever-optimistic Simon Cowell was already convinced that he had another number one.

The flip side was more difficult. "We wanted another established classic", said Robson. "One with superb structure, great melody and unforgettable lyrics. Another song about hope." Jerome suggested *Up On The Roof,* the song recorded by The Drifters (also in the 60s). Without any arguments ("the only time we ever have any heated discussion is usually over the choice of songs") the single had been decided and the release date fixed for October 30th. Now for the Christmas album. What should they call it? "How about Robson and Jerome's greatest hits", said Jerome. "You mean there's only going to be one track", replied Robson. "It's a joke, Rob, can't you see, it's a joke." This time there were a few disagreements but slowly the choice of songs for the album came together and it included *Danny Boy,* the song that Paddy Garvey sang to Nancy Thorpe on the evening he staggered across the parade ground and climbed a tree in the first series of *Soldier, Soldier.* The songs were exquisitely crafted by producer Nigel Wright who had worked with Barbara Streisand, Madonna and Michael Ball. "People may say we're old fashioned", said Robson, "but these songs have stood the test of time. Don't forget our audience is from from five to 95."

RCA decided that the video to accompany the single should be shot in New York so the boys (Robson for the first time) flew to America and, to the amusement of a few thousand Manhattans, were filmed in the streets, in the taxis, in Central Park and on the roof of a 53-storey skyscraper where they sang *Up on The Roof.* With them was producer Peter Bigg who remembered breathtaking views of the Chrysler and Pan Am buildings and no safety railing!

Back home the boys needed to rehearse the album songs so they got together in the back garden of Jerome's mum's home near Ide Hill. Fern remembers that

Jerome signing autographs at the Ide Hill village fair which he opened in the summer of 1995. He was mobbed and the village had never known anything like it as hundreds of female admirers queued for Jerome's autograph. He then handed out raffle prizes and told a few Tommy Cooper jokes as the organisers counted the profits from their most well-attended fair ever.

Sunday afternoon well. "They stood on the lawn singing along to the beat box. The neighbours were rather surprised when they heard a live performance from Robson and Jerome on the other side of the hedge."

In August Robson flew to South Africa to film his last few episodes of *Soldier, Soldier* and then suddenly had to fly home again. Television viewers had voted him the most popular actor in the country and he returned to attend the ceremony at Wembley with Alison, Jerome and Anna. Jerome also collected the National Television Award for the Most Popular Drama on behalf of *Soldier, Soldier*. Robson received his award from supermodel Claudia Schiffer and thanked the people who had started him off in acting and especially his former Live Theatre colleagues in Newcastle.

Robson's final episode showed the lads of 'B' Company caught up in an African civil war, crossing a mine field in an effort to keep one step ahead of rebel forces. In a most dramatic conclusion Dave Tucker was badly injured. "After five years it was the right time to move on", said Robson, "but I was sad to leave. *Soldier, Soldier* holds a special place in people's hearts."

I Believe/Up On The Roof was released on October 30th and Simon Cowell knew by the advance orders — 600,000 — that it would go into the charts at number one. It did. Following a tremendous publicity campaign it shot to the top easing aside Coolio, Queen and Meatloaf and once again Robson and Jerome went numb from a mixture of shock and excitement. Robson rang the record company every day of that week to check up on the sales figures. He said: "On Tuesday they described them as smashing, on Wednesday as ballistic and come Friday they said it was downright vulgar."

By the end of the first week *I Believe* had become the fastest selling single of the nineties, overtaking the previous highest, *Unchained Melody*. Jerome, keen as ever to play down the success, made it clear to the press corps who suddenly invaded his patch of East London that they were not taking any of it too seriously. "We were lucky that we could enjoy our singing because we didn't rely on it for our livelihood. I've always felt so sorry for those talented young musicians who are desperate for a break." This time Robson and Jerome topped the charts for four weeks and hovered in the top ten for a lot longer sending shock waves once again through the pop industry.

Jerome had a special mission in the summer of 1995. Not to save the whales or swim with a dolphin or to stop the nuclear testing in the Pacific, but to help raise £110,000 to send a three-year-old autistic boy to a special school in America. Jerome heard about the plight of Ben Simpson of Solihull and decided to help in the best way he could by trying to persuade the nation to recycle aluminium cans. He appeared on the programme Schofield's Quest with Ben's mother Julie and explained that aluminium cans worth £40 million are thrown away each year. A national campaign to have them recycled would not only raise the necessary money for Ben but save a valuable resource. Julie said: "The response from the public was so fantastic that we were able to consider building a special school for autistic children in England. I can't thank Jerome enough for his support. He's a great friend."

At the end of the fourth week the sales figures had shot up to 960,000 making the combined sales figures 2.8 million — the highest ever achieved by an act in its debut year and one of the highest of all time. They also became the first newcomers to have two singles in the top three in the same year since Adam Ant in 1981.

The showing of the fifth series of *Soldier, Soldier*, the regular appearances on Top of the Pops, more television interviews and more newspaper features were making it difficult for the boys to keep a low profile, especially Jerome who lived in Dalston. They were now household names and, according to the tabloids, sex symbols. "It's nice to be liked", said Jerome, "but it's ridiculous to call us sex symbols." Robson agreed: "The response was overwhelming and always positive. Guys on scaffolding, people in the corner shop and on the trains. Always complimentary. Never any hassle." The glare of publicity was doing wonders for the fan club and Kerry needed even more helpers in her Northumberland office to meet the demand for photo sets, T-shirts, sweatshirts and posters.

Robson and Jerome, the album, was released on November 13th. It emulated the two singles and went straight in at number one, selling more than 270,000 during the first week — the highest first-week sale ever achieved by a debut album. To the disgust of Oasis (and presumably many Oasis fans) who were displaced at the top of the album charts, the boys — who had never wanted to record a song at all — had made pop history. Could they now achieve what many said would be the impossible and keep The Beatles off the top when they released their much-publicised come-back album. The music industry and much of the country watched with anticipation.

It was hardly a contest. *The Beatles Anthology* went into the album charts at number two. Queen, with an unpublished Freddie Mercury album were somewhere below. For seven unbelievable triumphant weeks, however, Robson and Jerome were at the top and sold two million copies in the last 48 days of the year. They were the fastest two-million seller album ever. "Paul McCartney must have had mixed feelings", said Jerome. "He owned the rights to *Unchained Melody,* so we had already made almost a million pounds for his publishing company."

In the Top of the Pops studios, trying to look like pop stars.

This was a pop music success story almost without precedent. The blend of well-loved old favourites combined with the personal charm and popularity of two guys, already well-known by 17 million people, proved to have an appeal that suited all age groups. Robson and Jerome avoided over-sentimentality and it was that same fresh and almost

A moment from the filming of the video for Up on the Roof. There was a small storm brewing for the supposedly tranquil scene.

Robson and Jerome doing their Statue of Liberty impersonations. The video for Up on The Roof was made in New York with the dance sequence on top of one of the city's tallest buildings. The song was first recorded by the rhythm and blues vocal group, The Drifters in 1964. It was then used in a musical of the same name which opened at the Donmar Warehouse, London and transferred to the Apollo Theatre in June 1987. All the numbers in Up on The Roof were performed A Cappella and it received a nomination for the best musical.

apologetic quality that made their video such a success. Under Norman Stone's direction, *So Far So Good* became the biggest selling pop video in the hectic pre-Christmas selling period.

There were more chat shows and photo assignments to attend including one for *Hello* magazine and, an interview on Irish television in which Jerome was asked where the name Paddy Garvey came from. He told his story unaware that a researcher had tracked down the Irish boatman and the REAL Paddy Garvey was on the studio telephone waiting to talk from Dingle Bay.

Jerome: "Hello Paddy, it's me, Jerome." **Paddy Garvey:** (in his thick Irish brogue)... "Who?" **Jerome:** "Jerome Flynn, you remember me don't you?" **Paddy:** (long pause)... "No." **Jerome:** "You took me and my brother Dan out to see Fungi the dolphin four times on your boat, surely you remember?" **Paddy:** "No." **Jerome:** "Have you seen the series *Soldier, Soldier?*" **Paddy:** "No." **Jerome:** (getting slightly hysterical) "I borrowed your name for a television character in the series about the British Army. Did you know that?" **Paddy Garvey:** (slightly bewildered and not at all certain what this was about) "Oh... well... dat would explain why someone told me they saw my name in *Hello* magazine the other day."

The pinnacle of an extraordinary year came on November 20th when Robson and Jerome were invited to sing at the Royal Variety Performance in front of the Queen and the Duke of Edinburgh at the Dominion Theatre. It was a nerve-racking occasion, with Robson feeling desperately sick again but the host Des O'Connor, who had already interviewed the boys on his show, made them feel at ease and they sang *I Believe* in the first half of a programme. The Queen seemed to enjoy the show but her very presence meant she was missing her daughter-in-law's dramatic "Dianagate" television interview.

After the show the performers were introduced to the royal couple who chatted to them briefly. According to Robson the conversation went something like this. **Queen:** "Hello, you're on the telly, aren't you?" **Robson**: "Er, yes that's right." **Queen:** "Haven't you got a disc?" **Robson**: (silence). **Prince Philip:** "Hello, you're on the telly aren't you?" **Robson**: "Er, that's right." **Prince Philip:** "You've, um, er...got a bit of a disc, er sort of thing, haven't you?" Robson and Jerome exchange looks and smile. Philip moves on.

Two singles straight in at number one. An album straight in at number one. The highest first week sales ever. A video straight in at number one. The highest ever sales achieved in a debut year. The fastest two million seller ever. And now a sort of...er... chat with the Queen.

This really was the year of Robson and Jerome.

Chatting to the Queen and Prince Philip at the Royal Variety Performance

There was one more magic moment in a magic year for Robson and Jerome. A boyhood dream came true when they were both invited to play in a charity football match at Wembley in front of a huge crowd as a prelude to one of the big finals. "It was a crazy time", said Jerome. "It was a bit like being taken on a Disney theme ride of experiences. The real test was to remember we were just a couple of mates who had sung a song together. What happened after that wasn't down to us".

Robson with key members of his team of Beautiful Game. Left to right: Trevor Fox, Max Roberts (artistic director), Denise Welch (Marsha Stubbs in Soldier, Soldier), Robson and Peter Aughton, Theatre Royal General Manager.

The boys were invited to participate in a number of charity events during 1995 and, in one of them, Jerome was the backing singer for Michael Ball. In fact Jerome was returning a favour, because Michael had actually been his backing singer in a television advertisement for Budweiser beer some years previously. The filming for that commercial was made before Michael Ball shot into prominence to become Britain's number one recording artist.

FIRMLY established as the pop music sensations of 1995, Robson and Jerome went their separate ways in the early part of the New Year — Robson to Tyneside to set up his own production company and Jerome to India to continue his search for inner peace and the larger perspective.

Robson's beliefs in fair distribution and exchange of wealth — socialist principals inherited from a Geordie background and such influential voices as his paternal grandmother — were now being firmly established. Working hard during the winter months to set up his own company, Coastal Productions, Robson put aside money for a bursary to commission scripts and plays by local talent. He also donated £7,000 to Live Theatre to help improve the facilities which were so sadly lacking. "I understand what makes actors comfortable", he said, "and when I worked with the Live Theatre there were no proper changing rooms or shower facilities and no place to relax. In those precious, crucial moments before a performance I used to walk down the road to the quayside and sit on a seat by the Tyne river. It was my place for contemplation and relaxation. Now they have a proper dressing room."

Life for Robson had reached a peak. Apart from the music successes, the bursary and the fact that acting offers were flooding in almost every day, there was something happening down on the great arena of glorious turf, beloved by Tynesiders, called St James' Park, that was bordering on a miracle. Newcastle United, the Magpies, under the inspired managership of Kevin Keegan were leading the Premier Division of the Football League by a mile. Somewhere behind them were Manchester United and Liverpool. The title was there for the taking and the most passionate football supporters in the world were once more comparing Keegan's side with that of the glorious fifties. Robson and brother David and their dad were there regularly, although now as VIP guests of the chairman and on speaking terms with the players and staff.

The intensity of the new mood on Tyneside prompted Robson to invite Michael Chaplin to write a play centred around the history of Newcastle United to be performed in Newcastle in the summer of 1996. Everyone hoped, but hardly dared mutter the words, that *Beautiful Game* (as the play was called) would be an integral part of the Magpies' summer victory celebrations. But as the words were being created and the cream of the north-east acting talent was going up for auditions, Newcastle United hit a bad patch and the Cantona-brilliant Manchester United began to close the gap.

Only those who have watched football all their lives and followed one team through the ups and downs, seen talented players sold to keep the accounting books balanced and understood the fervour, the unity and companionship that the 'beautiful' game offers, will appreciate the agonies that Tynesiders now began to experience. Manchester United went ahead in the title race. Newcastle, with a game in hand, were in a position to catch them. Manchester won their final game and the Magpies entertained Spurs at St James' Park in an atmosphere of unbearable tension. They needed to win and win well. Even Jerome, a Spurs supporter for years, desperately wanted Newcastle to win because he knew how much it meant to Robson and the Geordie people.

Everyone knows the outcome. Spurs won giving the title (and eventually the double) to Manchester. Tyneside went into mourning and Robson returned to work with his Coastal Production team determined not to let the loss of a mere football title affect his enthusiasm for the new play, or the others he was planning. One was called *Dog Stars*, the story of a pub darts team from the northeast who travel to Germany to play a match that almost becomes another war. The other was *The Long Line*, the play with which Robson first made his mark and in which his father realised that his son was serious about an acting career.

Meanwhile Norman Stone — fascinated by the success and style of the video for *Unchained Melody* in which Robson and Jerome were seen following the two lovers from cinema to railway station — was having big ideas about making a film, set in 1940, that encompassed comedy, drama, music and romance. He felt more could be made of the Big Band sound of that period and, with the Robson and Jerome treatment and a good story-line, it could be ready for a 1996 revival. The boys, fired by Norman's enthusiasm, liked the idea of setting up a company to make a film in which they themselves starred and, with the big-ideas-man Norman on their side, there was never going to be a better opportunity than those heady days of late 1995. The result was Clapp Trapp Productions Ltd and the plot for the film actually materialised in Norman's head; in fact it was in a dream.

The film director had the ideal opportunity to tell his wife Sally Magnusson about the dream the following day when the couple were driving to a dinner party in Scotland. Sally, at the wheel, was mesmerised by the concept and, enthusiastically, added her own ideas. As the countryside flew by the plot began to take shape. The war years, a Battle of Britain hero injured, and medically discharged, and a Jack-the-lad avoiding conscription. Romance for one, scheming for the other. How they come together as singers in a big band. Gangsters, black-marketing and conflict in Blitz-torn London. Lots of comedy. War-time songs...By now Norman and Sally had taken a wrong turning on the motorway and were lost, somewhere in Scotland and miles off their chosen route. But that didn't matter. The story-line for a Robson and Jerome film was sound. Now they had to tell the boys and find a writer. Bob Larbey, who had created much-loved TV comedies such as *The Good Life* and *Ever Decreasing Circles,* was invited to turn those motorway-inspired thoughts into a musical comedy drama and the producer was to be George Gallaccio well known for *Bergerac* and other long-running series.

Norman, ever ambitious, now wanted a couple of living legends to take the part of the band leader and one of the principal jazz musicians. He invited Warren Mitchell, the actor inextricably identified with his portrayal of Alf Garnett in *Till Death us do Part* to play Ray Smiles. Warren, remembered also for his powerful performance as Willie Loman in *Death of a Salesman,* agreed. Now Norman approached George Melly, jazz singer and owner of a wide repertoire of violently coloured suits. Melly also accepted. To complete the principal performers Norman cast, as Dolly Nightingale, the stunning Julia Sawalha of *Absolutely Fabulous* and *Pride and Prejudice* fame. Within weeks co-stars in the shape of Jane Lapotaire, Jim Carter, James Cosmo and June Brown had been signed on, along with hundreds of extras. With a production bill already running into many hundreds of thousands of pounds, filming began at locations in London, Sussex and Wiltshire.

At RCA, Simon Cowell (like Norman Stone) was not going to let his heroes get away and quickly persuaded them to make another album for Christmas 1996 and a single for October.

In the recording studios for the 1996 triple-A single, What Becomes of the Broken Hearted? Saturday Night at the Movies and You'll Never Walk Alone, released in October.
You'll Never Walk Alone was composed by Richard Rodgers with lyrics by Oscar Hammerstein and was the inspirational climactic song in the musical Carousel. It was also recorded by the Liverpool beat group Gerry and the Pacemakers and was adopted by Liverpool as a football anthem. It was chosen months before the England successes in Euro 96 brought it again into public awareness

Eric on double bass. Eddie on the saxophone. The climax of the show. The song is Ain't Misbehavin'.

7: The Making of Ain't Misbehavin'

FILMING for the Norman Stone-conceived musical-comedy adventure epic began in April 1996 in London and then moved to the Blue Bell Railway in Sussex — the station and line rescued and restored by steam train enthusiasts. From there the moves were to the atmospheric Rivoli Ballrooms near Sydenham, a run-down candle factory yard near the Thames, an RAF base in Hampshire and finally to Chippenham, Wiltshire and the deepest, oldest and largest man-made underground cave system in the country where stone was originally excavated to build the city of Bath.

With so many fine actors, brilliant locations, extras numbering more than 100 and an excellent story-line there was only one thing missing — a good title. That evolved as filming progressed. One of the most evocative scenes was the moment when Robson and Jerome came together in the Ray Smiles Big Band to sing their version of the famous number *Ain't Misbehavin'*, a song that was also to be included in their next album. Because this

Eric and Eddie at the moment they first sang together with the Ray Smiles Big Band.

crucial moment in the film was accompanied by such a great wartime favourite, the song title was adopted for the film title. *Ain't Misbehavin'* was scheduled to be screened in three one-hour episodes on the ITV network as a winter special.

Once again the magic worked. The irresistible combination of the Green/ Flynn personalities set the piece alight. Many of the crew were familiar friends from the *Soldier, Soldier* days, and Norman Stone's charismatic personality made for a very happy working atmosphere on set – apart from the long working hours required from everybody.

Norman's magnificent ideas — A Blenheim bomber crash landing, a fifty piece band, authentic period costume for the huge cast including 82 extras in the Rivoli Ballroom, all cost a great deal of money. Robson and Jerome agreed to forego their salaries, temporarily, and invest their own money, such was their faith in Norman.

It was a move which could have cost them dear. As Norman kept saying, it was like investing the family silver; in Robson and Jerome's case the silver had only just arrived in the family cupboard! It was a worrying time for the two stars and their new Clapp Trapp Productions company.

The most important thing however was that they were enjoying working together again and the vibes from the viewing of the rushes were all good. As the production progressed through April into May the feeling went round that they had a winner on their hands, a feeling confirmed by the presence of the paparazzi who were lurking everywhere. On one London location there was a suspiciously open window above the street in which they were filming. Sure enough next day *The Sunday Mirror* carried an exclusive on the filming of the new show, albeit with rather distant shots of the two stars at work.

On another occasion at The Bluebell Railway Line station, an innocent German tourist was forbidden to take photographs of the steaming engines — he was surely a disguised member of the paparazzi — after all this was a film about wartime, and all foreigners were suspect. The poor man looked on in complete bewilderment as the filming continued but obediently kept his camera in its case.

Eventually it came to the final week's filming in the Chippenham area of Wiltshire, down that 'deep mine' and in Lady Wisley's stately home nearby. There was a romantic moment as Eddie Wallis (Jerome) sang to Dolly Nightingale from the shrubbery of the smoothly lawned garden. He reached the the last line "A nightingale sang in Berkeley Square"...You could hear a pin drop, and then a peacock screamed its unattractive cry in the still night air. Everybody collapsed into giggles.

Discharged from the RAF on medical grounds after his heroic crash-landing, Eddie Wallis takes a train to London on which he meets the gorgeous Dolly Nightingale, played by Julia Sawalha.

Jerome is Eddie Wallis, a former navigator with the RAF and man of principle who achieves national fame when he crash-lands a bomber single handed after a sortie over France. Injured in the incident, he is discharged from the RAF and pursues his only other career opportunity — that of a saxophone player in a Big Band.

Robson, as Eric Trapp, the son of Clara von Trapp, a faded Czech beauty, plays a Jack-the-lad character. Eric's great achievement is that he has managed to avoid conscription despite the fact that the police are looking for him. This dissolute charmer who deals exclusively in black market goods which he stores in his double-bass case, is also a member of the Ray Smiles Big Band.

*The legendary George Melly, who first sang with Mick Mulligan's jazz band in the late 1940's,
joined Robson and Jerome in Ain't Misbehavin', playing one of Ray Smiles' key resident jazz
singers. His disappearance from the scene leaves the way open for Eric and Eddie.*

Warren Mitchell is the Big Band leader Ray Smiles. Here he is with Eric Trapp, a hysterical scene with Robson on the maracas, doing his Spanish bit.

In real life they're The Shrinking Violets — an all-girl A Cappella group from North London. Here, in Ain't Misbehavin', they accompany the Ray Smiles band.

Robson and Jerome relax during filming at the candle factory yard in south London. Norman Stone enjoys the joke in the background.

When he is not singing Eric is a private detective. He has some hair-raising adventures.

THE most dramatic moment in the film, when Eddie Wallis and Eric Trapp are pursued by armed guardsmen, was also a real-life adventure for Robson and Jerome. With bullets rattling around them and the light fading fast Eric and Eddie scramble down a hillside, leap into their motor-cycle combination and realise that their only means of escape is across a river and over a hedge.

Robson had already made it clear that the stuntmen should perform this risky sequence. That's what they were paid for. But Jerome, hyped up and well into his character, said they could take over for the actual leap across the river. The director below the river bank would signal when to brake.

With no time for a rehearsal, Robson reluctantly climbed into the sidecar and hung on grimly as Jerome gathered speed. The bike screamed across the rain-sodden turf until it was time for Jerome to apply the brakes. But the wheels had locked and the bike started to skid towards the six-foot bank and the river below with Robson frantically trying to climb out of his moving coffin. The cameraman continued to shoot, recording genuine terror on Jerome's face.

It could have been a terrible tragedy but the bike came to a halt with the front wheel teetering over the bank and Jerome staring into the chasm. The camera crew ran to the rescue but by the time they had arrived Robson was already half way round the field screaming aloud. The whole of that near-fatal sequence appears unedited in the film for no-one could persuade Robson to do another take!

Robson is already frozen with fear as the motorbike careers across the field. "In this sequence", said Jerome, "neither of us were acting and everyone who watches Ain't Misbehavin' will realise that."

Robson relaxes and Jerome recovers from a lucky escape (as Eddie).

Discussing the Christmas album in the recording studios.

110

In uniform again for the making of Ain't Misbehavin'. Here they are seen at the entrance to the deep earth dump in Wiltshire, where the final day's filming took place.

The boys are in tune

I995 may have been the Year of Robson and Jerome but 1996 was no less hectic with the filming of *Ain't Misbehavin'*, a new single for the autumn, an album and a long-form video for Christmas, charity appearances and all the additional demands that seem to go hand in hand with stardom.

Robson spent the summer in Newcastle with his Coastal Prouction team working on his new plays including *Beautiful Game* which opened at the Theatre Royal in July. He also started work in August on a six-part TV drama *Reckless* for showing in 1997. Jerome was more relaxed, giving his private life a little more time and overseas trips, including one to Bosnia with the Red Cross where he spoke to children about mine awareness. Jerome has also been involved in developing an idea with Sean Blowers, an old friend from Central, for an ecological drama series.

The boys have declined to be drawn into too much discussion about the future. The way is open for both of them to return to *Soldier Soldier*, and that is a comforting thought for the fans, but unlikely to happen. They had five great series but ended up hardly able to talk to each other on camera, such was the leg-pulling and extraordinary jollity among the actors of the Kings' Own Fusiliers.

Norman Stone will not let them escape from the limelight, nor will Simon Cowell, if he has his way, or scores of casting directors or thousands of fans all over the country. They are almost certain to come together again, but in what form and how, we don't really know. Possibly, they might give in to one of numerous offers to go live — on the road. We may even see them singing at Wembley or The Albert Hall.

The Robson and Jerome story is one without an ending. It is a remarkable tale of two ordinary guys, one from the north-east, one from the south-east, who met for the first time in a popular TV drama and discovered, despite their contrasting upbringings that they shared many of the same tastes and many of the same passions. Most important was the passion for life and the need to celebrate it. That feeling was infectious and, from the ranks of the King's Own Fusiliers, it seeped out into 17 million British homes.

The boys themselves put their success down to luck. That may well be, but charisma has a big part to play and so has timing. Despite what all the critics may say, Robson and Jerome are in tune and certainly in tune with each other.

FROGLETS PUBLICATIONS, BRASTED CHART, WESTERHAM, KENT TN16 1LY: 01959 562972